Easter

Proclamation 4

Aids for Interpreting
the Lessons of the Church Year

Easter

Walter Brueggemann

Series A

FORTRESS PRESS   MINNEAPOLIS

PROCLAMATION 4
Aids for Interpreting the Lessons of the Church Year
Series A: Easter

Library of Congress Cataloging-in-Publication Data
(Revised for vol. 5–7, ser. A)

Proclamation 4.

Consists of 24 volumes in 3 series designated A, B,
and C, which corresponds to the cycles of the three year
lectionary. Each series contains 8 basic volumes with
the following titles: [1] Advent-Christmas, [2] Epiphany,
[3] Lent, [4] Holy Week, [5] Easter, [6] Pentecost 1,
[7] Pentecost 2, and [8] Pentecost 3. In addition there
are four volumes on the lesser festivals.
By Christopher R. Seitz and others.
Includes bibliographies.
1. Bible—Liturgical lessons, English. 2. Bible—
Homiletical use. 3. Bible—Criticism, interpretation,
etc. 4. Common lectionary. 5. Church year.
I. Seitz, Christopher R. II. Proclamation four.
BS391.2.S37   1989   264'.34   88-10982
ISBN 0-8006-4165-5 (Series A, Easter)

The paper used in this publication meets the minimum requirements of American National Standard for Information Sciences—Permanence of Paper for Printed Library Materials, ANSI Z39.48-1984. ∞™

Manufactured in the U.S.A.   AF 1–4165

93   92   91   90   89   1   2   3   4   5   6   7   8   9   10

Contents

The Resurrection of Our Lord
Easter Day

Lutheran	Roman Catholic	Episcopal	Common Lectionary
Acts 10:34–43	Acts 10:34a, 37–43	Acts 10:34–43	Acts 10:34–43 or Jer. 31:1–6
Col. 3:1–4	Col. 3:1–4	Col. 3:1–4	Col. 3:1–4 or Acts 10:34–43
John 20:1–9 or Matt. 28:1–10	John 20:1–9	John 20:1–10 or Matt. 28:1–10	John 20:1–18 or Matt. 28:1–10

In the texts for Easter Day, the Gospel reading is a *foundational story* of how the first believers came to new faith and new life. The epistle and reading from Acts are *reflections on the new life* to which we are summoned by the originary event. Preaching from these texts invites the congregation to reappropriate afresh the central conviction of Christian faith. That reappropriation is always twofold, always a *narrative remembering* of the first witnesses, and always *an ecclesiological, ethical reflection* on our new life.

Both the remembering and the reflection are essential. The narrative memory by itself may lead us only to wonder at the miracle, without noticing how it pertains practically to us. The reflection by itself may lead to new understanding of daily life, but without the authorizing, energizing testimony of the first witnesses. The narrative by itself may be irrelevant to our own life. The reflection by itself may be impotent. The two together are a powerful invitation for reappropriation. At its most effective, preaching from these texts may evoke a fresh embrace of the church's central conviction and identity. At the end of Easter Day, we may hope for a congregation newly authorized and energized for new life in the world, rooted in Jesus' own new life.

GOSPEL: JOHN 20:1-18

The Gospel reading is a narrative memory (one among many) of how the reality of Jesus' resurrection was mediated as faith in the church. The plot is set in v. 1. Mary Magdalene lacks any official role in the early church, but she keeps surfacing at crucial points in the narrative. She is the first one up on "the first day of the week" prepared to enact her devotion and loyalty to the dead Jesus. It is then she discovers the new fact that triggers the narrative—the stone is taken away (v. 1)!

Mary's testimony, inconclusive as it is, triggers the first action in the narrative (v. 2). She reports to "the leadership" of the community. Her tone suggests dismay. The body of the dead Jesus is misplaced, presumably dishonored. The "leadership" of course includes Simon Peter, the towering figure in the memory of the early church. His coming to the tomb is the arrival of the "official" church at the Easter miracle. There is perhaps a hint of jostling for power, as "the other disciple" gets there first (v. 4). The two may compete for priority at the tomb; both ignore Mary. Peter "saw" (vv. 6-7). The other disciple "saw and believed" (v. 8). The "other one" is the first one who comes to faith in the resurrection.

The narrative is wondrously reticent. We do not know and are not told how seeing led to believing. All the two saw was the emptiness and absence. What the "other disciple," "the one whom Jesus loved," believed, however, is of a different category. The one believed far beyond what the two saw. The two saw emptiness, the beloved one believed new life. In the odd, inarticulate moment which could have resulted in dismay, alienation and defeat, even without concrete evidence, there is faith. A church which has not yet understood its own Scripture comes to fresh faith (v. 9). There is no direct encounter with Jesus in this narrative with the two disciples, no speech by Jesus. Based on exceedingly thin evidence, the church believes!

Mary has been disregarded since her initial report. Now she reappears: "But Mary . . ." (v. 11). It is as though Mary had to wait her turn, until the "great ones" had finished. The narrative treats Mary with great attention. In contrast to the terseness of vv. 2-10, the narrative takes time to detail Mary's experience. The real meeting is not with "the great ones," but with this lowly, uncredentialed person. Her meeting at the tomb is freighted with more than the church can understand. There are two angels for her, as there were not for Peter (v. 12). Then (again as there was not for Peter) there is Jesus addressing her (v. 14)! Jesus is present for Mary, even if he is not yet recognized.

Twice Mary is asked, "Why are you weeping?" (vv. 13, 15). It seems unlikely that this is a question asked for information. Perhaps the question is a rebuke, for weeping is inappropriate to Jesus' new life and reflects her misreading of what has happened. Mary's response is still focused on the dead, misplaced, perhaps abused body of Jesus (v. 15). Mary knows no better. She knows nothing yet of the faith of the beloved disciple who has already departed.

The world-changing disclosure of Easter occurs for Mary in v. 16. The risen Jesus speaks again. He knows Mary. He addresses her; he calls her by name (cf. 10:3). He identifies her, summoning her to his new life. The act of naming is not only a disclosure of who Mary is, but also of who Jesus is. Now Jesus is recognized (v. 16). Mary answers, "Rabbi." Hers is a response of deference and yielding. Jesus is the one with authority, and she is prepared to be instructed. Jesus asserts his freedom and sovereignty to Mary (v. 17), and Mary is sent now with a more crucial and authoritative message (v. 18). Mary has seen and knows more than the disciples!

FIRST LESSON: ACTS 10:34-43

Chapter ten of Acts concerns Peter's witness to Cornelius, a Gentile. Cornelius is instructed by an angel to summon Peter (vv. 3-5). Peter is given a vision whereby he learns that God's concern is not limited to "the clean," that is, the Jews (vv. 11-15). Cornelius and his friends assemble to hear the preaching of Peter, who is now willing to engage the Gentiles.

The entire narrative of vv. 1-33 is stage-setting for Peter's preaching. The gospel is proclaimed in what is for Peter a strange context, among Gentiles to whom the old story of faith is as yet unknown. The power of the gospel, however, transforms that context for both Peter and Cornelius. Peter can now receive Cornelius, and Cornelius can now hear Peter. We are invited to share with those Gentiles in the hearing of Peter's sermon, to notice how the preaching of the resurrection may change life, as it did for those first hearers.

Peter's initial premise in v. 34 grows out of his vision in vv. 11-15. Those whom Peter regarded as "common" are admissible. All who listen to the word and obey are acceptable (vv. 34-35). There are no preconditions. The word preached is the story of Jesus, which is "good news of peace" to all who are oppressed and robbed of freedom (vv. 36-38). That peace is accomplished for all people by the purpose of God in the life of Jesus, without condition or qualification.

At the center of Peter's preaching is the resurrection (v. 40). In this text, however, we have to do not with the resurrection but with the *preaching of the resurrection*. The originary event of Easter has become the theme

and substance of preaching. In an extraordinary interpretation of the Easter
event, Peters casts this resurrection as a theocentric occurrence (vv. 40-
43). The resurrection is the means whereby God enacts forgiveness. The
new life of Jesus makes new life possible for those who believe (vv. 38-
39). "And we are witnesses" (v. 39). God's decisive action permits life in
the world to begin in a new way. Jesus' resurrection is the authorization
of God to the listeners to begin a new life, unencumbered, new life from
new power.

The response to Peter's sermon is the coming of the Spirit even to Gentiles
(vv. 44-46), the act of baptism (vv. 47-48), and thereby, the formation of
a new community. Cornelius and his friends do indeed hear. In response
to resurrection preaching, they break with all that is old. The listeners
break with their old life even as Peter the preacher has broken with his
old life. Easter preached evokes and permits new life. Peter's sermon forms
a new community which is morally, intellectually, and culturally liberated
from every old alienation. The ones who hear are forgiven and may begin
again.

EPISTLE: COLOSSIANS 3:1-4

The tale has been told (John 20:1-18). The power of newness has been
preached, resulting in baptism (Acts 10:34-43). Baptism authorized by
resurrection is a dramatic decision to begin life anew, accepted, forgiven,
and at peace. Baptism that begins life again, however, also places one in
crisis, confronted by demanding decisions, yearning for new life, attracted
to or seduced by the power of the old age. The Epistle to the Colossians,
in glorious, lyrical language, responds to the question: What happens if
you are baptized into this new faith and new power? In baptism we are
already raised to new life.

It will take some imaginative work in a typical North American congregation, which views Easter with a bit of nostalgic magic, but the task
of preaching this text is to show that resurrection, dramatized and enacted
by baptism, is a current event in our life. Thus the urgent issue of Easter
is not the conventional question of how would a dead man come out of a
tomb. Our question rather is, How is the new life given us in the gospel
to be actualized and enacted in our own daily context?

In Colossians 3, the language of "put to death" (v. 5) and "put on then"
(v. 12) is a baptismal formula. In the dramatic act of baptism, one changes
from old life to new life, even as one changes from old clothes to new
clothes. The baptismal formula in our epistle reading utilizes the metaphor

of changing clothes: "put on then" (3:12), that is, put on new clothes, habits, and practices befitting new life, just as we have put to death what is old (3:5). (The two formulations of 3:5, 12 are not symmetrical as they are in Eph. 4:22-24, but the point is the same.)

Thus our text articulates two parallel sets of formulae characterizing the new situation of the believer because of the gospel. The first set of formulae concerns crucifixion and resurrection of the believer who identifies with Jesus:

(a) If with Christ you have died . . . (2:20),

   } our death and resurrection.

(b) If you have been raised . . . (3:1)

The second set of formulae concerns baptism which enacts for the believer the reality of crucifixion and resurrection:

(a) Put to death . . . (3:5),

   } our baptism into new life.

(b) Put on then . . . (3:12)

Both sets of formulae affirm that a decisive change has been wrought in our lives by the drama of the gospel.

It now remains in the church to give intentional, practical expression to the new status given us in resurrection and in baptism. The double imperative of our text is expressed in spatial imagery:

Seek the things that are above (v. 1),
Set your minds on things that are above (v. 2).

The spatial imagery, however, is filled with theological substance (cf. John 20:17). The spatial imagery of the heavenly throne might be rendered: "Seek what is appropriate to Christ; set your mind on what is congruent with the character of God."

The spatial imagery articulates a profound moral requirement, given specificity in the catalogues of vv. 5 and 12. The baptized are to relinquish whatever is marked by "immorality, impurity, passion, evil desire, and covetousness which is idolatry" (v. 5). The new life is marked by "compassion, kindness, lowliness, meekness, and patience . . . forgiving one another" (vv. 12-13). The power of the resurrection and the summons of baptism together make new life possible. Those who adhere to the resurrection are to live, giving evidence that the passions, compulsions, and gods of an unresurrected, unbaptized world no longer have force or authority in their lives. The new life of the resurrected, baptized community is not a narrow vision of personal purity, but an ethical posture that touches every domain of life. The text obviously asserts not new rules, but power for transformed living.

The new life of the baptized community depends on power that the world cannot see, and to which the world has no access. Our life is hid with Christ in God (v. 3), hid beyond analysis, kept safe by the same inscrutable power that transformed a dead Jesus into a living Lord. Finally, it is promised that Christ's rule will be fully established (v. 4). Those who have embraced new life will stand with him, free, healed, and joyous in the very presence of God (v. 4). The text remarkably combines lyrical anticipation and concrete requirement.

In these texts there is a sequenced coherence from *resurrection* (John 20:1-18) to *preaching* (which leads to baptism) (Acts 10:34-43), to *new life* (Col. 3:1-4). The Gospel narrative is a confrontation with the new life of Jesus which defies our explanation. His new life is a holy event breaking beyond our covenantal categories. The earliest witness of Mary led to the preaching of the resurrection by Peter, who is also a witness. Peter's powerful testimony summons Cornelius and all "outsiders" to baptism and new life. Baptism in turn raises issues about conduct and life-style that must be given concrete expression. The sequence of *resurrection-preaching-new life* means that the Easter event has weighty, inescapable moral content for us.

All three texts are aimed at the same crisis. Mary, the beloved disciple Peter, and the early church must decide about the new life of Jesus. Cornelius and his friends must decide about the new forgiveness. The Colossian church must decide about the elemental spirits that tempt and seduce (2:20), and about the liberated alternative of the gospel.

We, like Cornelius and the Colossians, do indeed yearn for another way of living. In these texts is an offer of another life rooted in the very power of God, given with concreteness for our daily life. What might happen in this sermon is that Easter is no longer seen as an ancient "spring rite" or a dazzling supernatural act, but the most powerful promise and the most subversive summons we have ever faced. The promise and the summons hold out an odd gift of peace that is offered nowhere else!

Easter Evening
or Easter Monday

Lutheran	Roman Catholic	Episcopal
Dan. 12:1–3 *or* Jon. 2:2–9	Acts 2:14, 22–32	Acts 5:29a, 30–32 *or* Dan. 12:1–3
1 Cor. 5:6–8		1 Cor. 5:6b–8 *or* Acts 5:29a, 30–32
Luke 24:13–49	Matt. 28:8–15	Luke 24:13–35

FIRST LESSON: DANIEL 12:1-3

The book of Daniel is at the extreme edge of Old Testament faith. It articulates faith for God's people in an exceedingly dark moment when the forces of evil seem to have triumphed in the historical process. A hostile political force, the Seleucids, are intent on crushing Judaism. There seems not much that good men and women can do to maintain a faithful community. That situation of defeat, however, does not lead Israel to despair or resignation. Instead, it leads Israel to more daring, passionate faith. In the darkness, Jews are cast more completely upon the sovereignty of God, trusting that when human effort cannot deter evil, the relentless rule of God will prevail in the face of evil. God's power is trusted even against the massive power of death.

In the midst of an enormous darkness (the darkness of persecution), our text bursts into the life of faith with power and freshness. When everything on earth seems to have failed, there is an intrusion. Michael, prince among the angels of God, enters the world of the faithful. He comes from the government of God to fulfill the intent of God which the power of evil cannot defeat (v. 1). The text is cast in the apocalyptic rhetoric of the ultimate struggle of God with evil.

There will be a time of deep, deep "trouble" (v. 1). It will be the worst of times, the time when God's faithful are abused. That same moment of deep trouble will, however, be the time of deliverance for the faithful. All those who are faithful, all those who keep the disciplines, all those in the trusting community, will be delivered. Even in this extremity, Israel continues to promise and expect rescue from God. The text recasts an historical crisis into a great cosmic assertion of God's power and fidelity.

The promised rescue in Israel needs to be more decisive and more sweeping than any deliverance known heretofore in Israel. Thus in this text, the faith of Israel presses to a new form of imagination. It dares to suggest that the drama of rescue has now pushed out beyond the normal bounds of historical experience. Rescue now takes the form of resurrection from the dead. God's rescue did not happen in time to save from death. But Michael and the government of God are not defeated by the coming of death. God's rescue will reach even those who seem beyond rescue.

Moreover, this rescue by way of resurrection is ethically serious and exacting. The text does not envision a general, indiscriminate rescue. All shall awake, some to everlasting life and some to everlasting contempt. The moment of resurrection is a moment of ominous adjudication, in which one's future follows from one's faithfulness. The sweeping vision of these verses does not at all relax the moral seriousness of Jewish tradition. In this life and in the life to come, obedience to the purpose of God matters decisively. Thus the text provides a linkage between the inscrutable mystery of resurrection and the urgency of responsible obedience.

The good promise of the resurrection is for the faithful. In v. 3, they are termed "wise." They are the ones who have been obedient and true, who have not compromised or accommodated themselves to the power of evil. They have been righteous and they have turned many others to righteousness. Their reward and consolation is that they will be as bright, shining, beautiful, and valued as the very stars; they shall live as long and as splendidly as the stars shine (v. 3).

It is obvious that preaching from this text is problematic. On the one hand, the text is an intellectual affront with its image of judgment and its metaphor of Michael. On the other hand, the text is easily distorted as the voice of "hellfire and damnation." There is nonetheless urgency and importance in proclaiming this text. The preacher need not, in my judgment, spend much energy accommodating modernity or adjusting this text to our rationality. It is more useful to give voice to this outrageous vision of a coming accountability, not by way of threat, but as hope. The text invites us to reflect upon and affirm the following:

1. Our life is not headed toward dismal defeat, but toward the powerful, good rule of God.
2. The world is not morally indifferent, but lives that are caring and discerning are ultimately valued.
3. The world is not resignedly handed over to brutality and inhumanity, but the power of good is at work in decisive ways.

God's power is at work; therefore, the faithful may hope in every circumstance. While hoping, the faithful can be zealously and passionately obedient.

GOSPEL: LUKE 24:13-49

The opening of the narrative (vv. 13-14) sets the scene, but tells us very little. Two of the apostles (who are not named) are leaving Jerusalem, the scene of the final "showdown" for Jesus. They were discussing "all these things," but we are not told what things. Everything is held in abeyance in the narrative, awaiting the arrival of the "main character." In v. 15, the main character arrives. The conversation between the unnamed apostles and the unrecognized Jesus can be treated in three scenes:

(a) 24:15-24. This long scene offers an extended conversation that keeps Jesus hidden, so that the disciples do not recognize him. "Their eyes were kept from recognizing him" (v. 16). The men (like the women at the tomb, v. 24), did not see. The conversation is an unequal one. Jesus is lord of the conversation, but is unrecognized as sovereign. Jesus initiates the conversation. He makes it possible for the apostles to retell the story of his death and resurrection. In their retelling, the witnesses say more than they understand.

The witnesses present the basic conflict between the great prophet (v. 19) and the "priests and rulers" who oppose him (v. 20). Jesus is in a mighty conflict with the rulers of this age, and he has been defeated. His defeat terminated the hope of the apostles. "We had hoped" (v. 21). They had read the promise of Daniel and they had expected the triumph of God's rule for Jesus, the righteous one. That triumph, however, had not happened. The first outcome of the Christian story is the failure of Jesus and the defeat of God. These apostles hope only in the past tense.

Verses 22-24 begin with an abrupt adversative: "But." Against the conviction of death, against the evidence at hand, there is amazement (v. 22). Jesus' death seemed final, but the experience of the women contradicts that finality. The women saw and heard angels (v. 23). Clearly, this is no ordinary story. It is not a narrative congenial to our technical epistemology. It is a story fraught with imagination, peopled with voices that belong, not to normal perceptions of reality, but to the inscrutable experience of theophany. The women were amazed. Their odd testimony was checked out by "some of those who were with us" (v. 24), that is, apostles. The women had seen angels, but the apostles "did not see." What was disclosed to the women was withheld from the ones who were authorized to give verification. The testimony of the women remains amazing, but unverified.

On the road, the two are conversing about a factual defeat and a rumored triumph. The two parts of the story are unequal in their force. The narrative has thus far precluded any present tense action. The two apostles are preoccupied with reported and removed events elsewhere (v. 24). They do not notice their own moment in the conversation with Jesus.

(b) 24:25-27. In the second phase of the conversation Jesus breaks off the bewildered tale of the apostles before they finish (vv. 25-27). Jesus does not linger over the unconfirmed testimony of the women, or their fragile, doubting amazement. He draws attention to the present moment. He wants the two men to pay attention to their own "resurrection experience," which does not depend on other testimony. He wants them to acknowledge their own present tense time with the risen, living Jesus. He rebukes them: "Are you so stupid and inattentive that you do not notice (v. 25)?" The events of Jesus are not unexpected or isolated. The entire Jewish tradition has pointed to this sequence of massive defeat and amazement. Then, says the narrative, the unrecognized Jesus reinterprets the whole Old Testament from the perspective of crucifixion and resurrection (v. 27). The faith of Israel is about the sovereign reversal of life which is now enacted in Jesus. The apostles "had hoped." Jesus answers with impatience; the whole hope of Israel is actualized in these events of defeat and amazement. They had failed to recognize Jesus, and they had failed to understand their own tradition of faith.

(c) 24:28-32. After the conversation which tells the story (vv. 19-24) and after the rereading of the tradition (vv. 25-27), Jesus enacts the Eucharist with the disciples (v. 30). After exegesis comes sacrament. Jesus utters the four dominical words: "took, blessed, broke, gave." No doubt the casting of the narrative mirrors the eucharistic practice of the early church. The events of the crucifixion and resurrection are now sacramentally reiterated; the brokenness enacted and spoken by Jesus is a witness to the breaking of Jesus (crucifixion) and the giving of life (resurrection). The

sacramental practice mediates, makes available, and discloses the odd meaning of breaking and feeding which the apostles had failed to discern.

This eucharistic moment is not routinized ritual. It is a moment of revelation. Their best-known but undeciphered tale is now made available to them as transformative news. Their eyes are opened! They recognized him (v. 31)! We have come a long distance from their unresponsiveness in v. 16. Indeed, the story concerns their move from not recognizing (v. 16) to recognizing (v. 31), a move which required reentry into the tradition, and the odd sacrament of defeat and amazement. The disciples now know, understand, and recognize. They now know because the risen one "has drawn near" (v. 15). They had hoped; now they have received. They can again hope present tense.

The conclusion of the narrative (vv. 33-35) is a counterpart to the beginning (vv. 13-14). The encounter of the disciples with Jesus causes an abrupt turn in their journey. Immediately, abruptly, "that same hour," they return to Jerusalem and to the community of disciples they had left (v. 33). They have now seen what was hidden. They have now recognized that one who had been unrecognized. They have now verified what was rumored. They are brimming with excitement, eager to hear news of what they now know.

Their eagerness notwithstanding, their news is preempted. When they return to the company of the disciples, they do not get to speak. They must listen (v. 34). The travelers thought they would give the news, but instead the news is given to them, "from the highest authority." It is none other than Simon who is cited as the authenticator of the news (v. 34). Two things are odd about this testimony. First, the witness of the women is disregarded, as though they are not important witnesses (cf. vv. 10-11). Second, we have no account in Luke of an Easter appearance of Jesus to Peter. Nonetheless, it is Peter's witness that counts. We can see how the initial news has been shaped by the authority and claims of the church. It is the authorized church which is the verifier and trustworthy witness to the surprise of the gospel.

Only after this decisive assertion on the authority of Simon do the men from the journey present their vision of the news (v. 35). There is some deliberate tension in the narrative between the abrupt claim of Peter's witness and the less direct news that has come from the Eucharist. In that single exchange between the travelers and the ones in Jerusalem, the text holds together two ways in which the early church has witnessed and believed.

The two men have had a strange encounter indeed. It has been a journey of new exegetical interpretation (v. 27) and of sacramental awareness (vv. 30-31, 35). In word and in sacrament, the daily practice of the church is the primal witness to the new life of Jesus. The church, by the end of this narrative, is no longer in doubt or defeat. It is energized to new faith. In our hearing the narrative, we are invited to the same faith, hope, and energy. The retelling of this account, the rereading of Scripture, and the celebration of broken bread are the ways in which the risen Jesus is known in the church.

EPISTLE: 1 CORINTHIANS 5:6-8

Paul is concerned for the moral passions of the congregation in Corinth. That church was characteristically bold and self-confident. It lived at the brink of moral arrogance. The case in point in our text is incest (v. 1). The debate which follows, however, is not about the affront of incest. Paul is concerned that the community might tolerate the offender and so jeopardize the purity and effectiveness of the community. Paul summons the church to live a life congruent with the power of the gospel.

The argument of our verses is difficult, because the metaphor of "leaven" is used in several different ways in these verses. The premise is that a little leaven will leaven the whole lump of dough (v. 6). In this pastoral case, the one offender will defile the entire community. (One bad apple will spoil the whole barrel.)

On the basis of that premise in v. 6., v. 7 issues an imperative that the community must eliminate the offender for the sake of the community. Paul urges that the old leaven (offender) be removed in order that the community may be a new, purified lump of dough. Thus in v. 7, the metaphor of leaven has shifted to speak about old and new (old lump, new lump, old community, new community, old impurity, new obedience). The new faithfulness is contrasted with old faithfulness, not as old leaven and new leaven (as might be expected from v. 6), but as leavened and unleavened. The community is to be radically new (and pure) according to the newness of the gospel.

The reference to Passover in v. 7a should not surprise us. Two themes emerge which speak of Jesus as the lamb of the Passover. On the one hand, there is the contrast between the unleavened bread of Passover and other bread which is leavened. On the other hand, Jesus is the new Passover in contrast to the old Passover, and so a new joy and a new obedience are offered. The contrast of old/new is extrapolated to a broader ethical teaching

(v. 8). The old leaven is malice and evil, categories that are more general than the specific case of incest. The new unleavened bread is sincerity and truth.

Verse 8 thus draws a conclusion which brings the metaphor back to the concreteness of the Corinthian crisis. The metaphor is now explicitly interpreted so that old leaven is marked by distorted conduct (murder, evil), while the new unleaven is appropriate to the new Passover as sincerity and truth.

The complex argument of vv. 1-8 thus is the following:

(a) moral crisis (vv. 1-5);

(b) mediation by a metaphor (vv. 6-7);

(c) moral crisis illuminated by metaphor (v. 8).

The completed argument is a call for new, purified behavior in the community of faith.

The convergence of these three texts is odd and not obvious. I suggest, however, that the texts together voice two different relations between resurrection and new obedience:

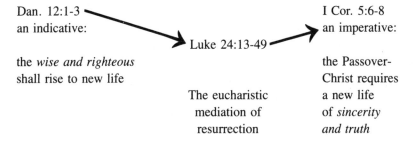

Dan. 12:1-3
an indicative:

Luke 24:13-49

I Cor. 5:6-8
an imperative:

the *wise and righteous*
shall rise to new life

The eucharistic
mediation of
resurrection

the Passover-
Christ requires
a new life
of *sincerity
and truth*

The ethical components of Dan. 12:3 (wise, righteous) and 1 Cor. 5:6-8 (sincerity, truth) are rough equivalents. Thus both the pre-Gospel text (Daniel) and the post-Gospel text (epistle) focus on ethical requirements. In the former, obedience leads to a certain kind of resurrection. In the latter, resurrection summons to obedience. Between the two texts concerning obedience is placed the awesome, inscrutable meeting with the risen Jesus who permits new life to begin (the Gospel narrative). Israel hopes for the resurrection (Dan. 12:2). The disciples had specifically hoped in Jesus (Luke 24:21). Now that hope of Israel is enacted in the life of the church. The enacted hope of new life permits new, obedient living. The convergence of these three texts presents the miracle of Easter as an impetus for new life in the world. The four ethical terms of *wise, righteous,* (from

Daniel) *sincere, truth* (from 1 Corinthians) touch every aspect of life. Christians perceive the world differently because of the resurrection and are authorized to act differently.

The Second Sunday of Easter

Lutheran	Roman Catholic	Episcopal	Common Lectionary
Acts 2:14a, 22–32	Acts 2:42–47	Acts 2:14a, 22–32	Acts 2:14a, 22–32
1 Pet. 1:3–9	1 Pet. 1:3–9	1 Pet. 1:3–9	1 Pet. 1:3–9
John 20:19–31	John 20:19–31	John 20:19–31	John 20:19–31

GOSPEL: JOHN 20:19–31

The first part of John 20 (vv. 1-18), our Easter Day reading, purports to narrate the original experience and witness of Mary, Peter, and "the other disciple." The second part of the chapter (vv. 19-31) turns to a different problem: How can this originary event continue to have power and authority beyond the first immediate witnesses? How does the reality of the resurrection continue to evoke and legitimate faith in the church? The answer of the Fourth Gospel is that these signs "are written that you may believe . . . may have life in his name" (v. 31). The evangelist proposes that it is *the text* (the writing) that mediates faith to subsequent generations of believers. Thus the preacher may concern herself with our interpretive problem of Easter: How shall we, with this text in hand, now appropriate the reality of the resurrection as our own experience?

The Gospel lection provides two vignettes for this "overcoming of historical time." First (vv. 19-23), the risen Jesus comes where the doors were shut (v. 19). This odd appearance of Jesus is not a scene from the movie *Poltergeist*. It rather concerns the lively, sovereign presence of Jesus who is known to be present where his presence is thought to be impossible.

No wonder the disciples are frightened (v. 19). Because of their odd faith, they lived in a hostile environment; they had withdrawn from public life in order to keep themselves safe. The door in the narrative is of course a concrete reference. It may also be taken as a metaphorical reference to all barriers whereby the church seeks to shut out the threat of the world and protect itself. The text is terse and elusive (v. 19). It does not explain Jesus' entry, nor is it troubled about his intrusion. It only bears witness to Jesus' sovereign presence and speech. Jesus speaks his lordly blessing, "peace" (v. 19). He brings peace to a frightened community which thinks it has been abandoned. This one who violates boundaries and overrides barriers of fear transforms the situation of his followers with an offer of peace.

Immediately, the narrative turns from the wonder of the living Lord to the mission of the church (v. 21). Three aspects of the word of the risen Christ may be noted: *(a)* The church is sent, as Jesus is sent (v. 21). The church is not permitted either to wallow in its fear and resourcelessness, nor to luxuriate in its risen lord. It is promptly dispatched in mission. *(b)* This sent church is not only under the rule of Christ who is risen; it is visited immediately by the Holy Spirit who guides, guards, and instructs (v. 22). The church does not possess a constantly visible Jesus, but it is given a gift of power. *(c)* The missional business of the church is forgiveness (v. 23). This forgiveness is not cheap, careless, or romantic. Sins may indeed by "retained." The church, however, must accept the crisis and burden of forgiveness as its central mandate. That is its purpose.

The second episode is equally ecclesiological and more pointed about the problem of subsequent generations of believers (vv. 24-29). In this narrative, Thomas embodies all those (and all those generations) who could not be present for the initial astonishment of the resurrection. In its elemental testimony, the church asserts, "We have seen the Lord" (v. 25, cf. v. 18). That initial testimony, however, is not taken at face value by Thomas; it must have been often doubted. Thomas responds with skepticism: "Show me" (v. 25).

Thomas, however, is not merely skeptical. He embodies the great catholic tradition of faith that eschews every gnostic, idealist, romantic notion of a "Christ figure" who floats above historical reality. Thomas is not a doubter, but one who insists on historical concreteness, who regards as urgent the fact that the risen Christ is indeed the one who was crucified. Indeed, this continuity of the dead one and the living one is crucial for faith, and Thomas insists on this continuity.

In this narrative Jesus does not resist the urging of Thomas (v. 27; cf. v. 20). No fifth amendment is taken by Jesus. The narrator tells of the reality of Jesus' wounds. The astonished disciples are indeed in the presence of the one who has been crucified. The doubt of Thomas is presented as a close parallel to the meeting of vv. 19-23. In both accounts, the marks of suffering are exhibited. In both episodes, Jesus speaks: "Peace" (v. 26). The suffering Jesus has become the basis of the possibility of peace. Jesus' pain points toward wholeness. That is why Thomas's insistence is crucial: The wounded one is the one who gives life.

Thomas believes (v. 28)! He confesses: "My Lord and my God!" In this confessional formula the church voices its conviction that Jesus is the risen Christ. Jesus is the dead one raised. The confession is crucial for Christology. The confession is no less crucial for ecclesiology. Certitude about Jesus permits Thomas to move beyond his doubt to a life of glad obedience. The gift of the Spirit (which is the breath of Jesus, v. 22) moves beyond the historical Jesus to the continuing power of God in the life of the church. Now the church must rely not on the *body of Jesus* (which is scarred and hurt), but on the *word of Jesus* ("Peace," vv. 19-26), and on the *breath of Jesus* (v. 22), which surprises and empowers. In this one episode, the Fourth Gospel summarizes the entire account of "the church under the Spirit," a theme fully explicated in the Book of Acts. The risen Jesus authorizes the church for its work.

By the end of this chapter, we are a long way from Mary's initial witness on Easter morning (v. 18) and from the disciples who have seen (vv. 6-8). We share Thomas's confession. We are a part of that community that is "sent" (v. 21), whose business is forgiveness (v. 23). This text narrates and enacts the mandate and faith of the church out beyond the initial event of resurrection, believing where it cannot see.

FIRST LESSON: ACTS 2:14a, 22-32

This sermon of Peter is addressed to the "men of Israel" (v. 22). It builds its argument by references and allusions to the well-known Jewish memory of faith. The core of Peter's proclamation is a quick rendering of the death and resurrection of Jesus (vv. 22-24). Four points tell what most needs to be told about Peter's sermon:

• Jesus did signs and wonders that are already known (v. 22). The story of Jesus' transformative life and ministry are summarized.

• The story of Jesus is theocentric. All of the events about Jesus belong to the plan and intention of God: "attested by God, delivered up . . . by God, God raised him up." (vv. 22-24). The narrative plot of the gospel is larger than Jesus. It concerns God's will for the world.

• The crucifixion of Jesus happened, even if by God's plan, at the hands of "lawless men" (v. 23). Such lawless action marked by brutality none-theless serves God's intention.

• Peter's proclamation centers in the wonder of the resurrection. God raised Jesus up (v. 24) according to God's plan, in opposition to the destructive work of the "lawless."

The imagery of the verse seems to be drawn from Israel's conventional rhetoric of complaint psalms. When one describes in prayer one's desperate situation, one is portrayed as caught in something like seaweed that catches, chokes, and binds, until one is helpless (cf. Pss. 18:4-5; 116:3). The image of cords of the pit and the snares of Sheol are used to speak of the power of evil and death, a power that renders the suppliant helpless and hopeless. That image of helplessness and hopelessness is applied to Jesus. He was caught in the power of death. He really was dead, left hopeless!

But God loosened him, broke the grip of seaweed, tore lose the cords, ended the helplessness and set him free (v. 24)! It is impossible to keep Jesus dead or immobilized. God's plan for a lively, life-giving Jesus is set against the brutal power of death. God is stronger than all those powers that would confine or nullify Jesus.

We are here at the crucial and difficult center of the gospel. God's power for life is so strong, so massive, so irresistible, so determined, that it generates force and energy against the most powerful restrictions imaginable. Death is portrayed as a power that imprisons, ensnares, and renders one helpless. That power for death, however, is not ultimately powerful. It is not possible for death to contain or resist the power of God. God's greater power and lively resolve cause Jesus to be free and alive!

As v. 24 alludes to the complaint psalms to describe the trouble of death, vv. 25-28 are a direct quote from Psalm 16:8-11, which is a glad song of thanksgiving celebrating rescue. Peter's sermon is saturated with the psalms. Psalms of complaint (in v. 24 by allusion) and gratitude for rescue (in vv. 25-28 by direct quote) are juxtaposed in order to speak of Jesus' situation of death and new life. The juxtaposition of complaint and confidence sets God's massive power over against the power of death (vv. 24-28). As Israel's complaint ends in thankful trust, as ensnarement ends in liberation, so the death of Jesus has ended in his new life.

Verses 29-31 provide an important interpretive reflection on the argument just stated. The verses concern royal theology. The family of David carries the promise of God that has not failed (cf. 2 Sam. 7:14-16). Jesus is the fulfillment of that promise and is the true David. Jesus is an enactment

of the royal promise that endures by the faithfulness of God, long after
the death of David. The verses do not advance the point made in vv. 22-
24, but provide a supportive argument for the identification of complaint
with crucifixion, thanksgiving with resurrection.

The climactic statement of v. 32 returns to the central claim of v. 24.
God raised Jesus and we are witnesses. Peter's sole, simple point is to
witness to the power of God for life in the liberation of Jesus from death.

The "men of Israel" are invited to embrace the new reality wrought in
that act of power. We are not told what such an embrace may entail. Peter
invites his listeners to the new power and the new social reality generated
by the resurrection. Peter's preaching invites his listeners to experience,
as did Jesus, the choking, debilitating power of death—and to begin again.

EPISTLE: 1 PETER 1:3-9

The epistle is addressed to those who experience hardship for the sake
of their faith. In eloquent phrases the passage posits an intense, decisive
connection between present faith and future hope.

The hope is rooted in the resurrection of Jesus (v. 3). As speech about
God's future must always be, the language is imprecise, lyrical, and open-
ended. God's power for life promises to the faithful a good, joyous outcome
in the end. That promised end, "in heaven," "in the last time" (vv. 4-5),
is guaranteed; it will not be spoiled and cannot be denied (v. 4). It is sure.

The faithful who act out their faith for "a little while" will suffer various
trials (v. 6). In the world of the Roman empire, we may imagine that such
faith required standing firm against popular opinion, with some risk and
some persecution. We are given no specifics, but the present tense of faith
was costly and demanding.

The linkage between future hope (vv. 3-5) and present faith (vv. 6-7) is
love of Jesus whom you have not seen (v. 8). The text brings us back to
Thomas in the Gospel reading and to the post-Thomas situation when faith
is required beyond sight. The faithful, troubled church is asked to trust in
Jesus and the power of the resurrection, even though the visible presence
of Jesus is no longer available.

The connection between faith and hope, between present endurance and
future expectation, is an urgent one in our time, as in every time. The
gospel calls the faithful to stand in hard, costly, and demanding places
against dominant opinion, certainly as much against the "ideology of the
empire" as in ancient days. The reality of a future promise is an incentive
for courage in the present.

These three texts cohere in their urgent invitation to trust in the power of new life when the concrete person of Jesus is no longer available. The circle of disciples after Thomas, the men of Israel addressed by Peter, and the diaspora in the letter of Peter are all summoned to the same faith, to believe when we cannot see, to accompany when we cannot touch, to trust what is only a promise. The power of death is tough and resilient. Against that power, the church has these originary witnesses to Jesus' new life on which it stakes everything.

In all three texts, the reality of the living Jesus is affirmed and assumed, not argued. The real stress point, however, is the response that must be made. The world, which resists the witness to the resurrection, submits to the power of death. We are so habituated to those "cords and snares," we can hardly imagine a liberating alternative. These texts summon preachers as daring as Peter, and congregations as responsive as his listeners must have been. The church continues to be summoned by daring, fragile testimony in the face of old, entrenched powers. Those old powers in fact have no power, cannot keep promises, and cannot give life. These daring witnesses point to another power, present in Jesus, that yields life.

The Third Sunday of Easter

Lutheran	Roman Catholic	Episcopal	Common Lectionary
Acts 2:14a, 36–47	Acts 2:14a, 22–33	Acts 2:14a, 36–47	Acts 2:14a, 36–41
1 Pet. 1:17–21	1 Pet. 1:17–21	1 Pet. 1:17–23	1 Pet. 1:17–23
Luke 24:13–35	Luke 24:13–35	Luke 24:13–35	Luke 24:13–35

FIRST LESSON: ACTS 2:14a, 36-47

Peter continues his preaching to the men of Israel (v. 14). Just before our lesson, Peter has issued his summary statement about the resurrection (v. 32). Now he draws a theological, christological conclusion (v. 36). The statement is theocentric; God has acted. It is not "Jesus has become," but "God has made." God's action transforms the crucified one into "Lord and Christ." This text asserts that Jesus was not "Lord and Christ" until after the crucifixion. This text treats resurrection as enthronement or exaltation. Jesus now is ruler and messiah, that is, the one promised long ago by God to enact the new kingdom promised in Israel. The one who was ruler is the very one who is crucified. The dead one is not only the live one, but the live one who must now be obeyed.

Peter does not linger over the problem of how to get from death to life, from Friday to Sunday. Peter is not a philosophic theologian. He is a "witness" (v. 32). He can only and need only tell the truth as he has discerned it. The truth is that Jesus was not defeated or destroyed, but governs. That is the end of the sermon. It is the classic Christian sermon. The sermon mobilizes the entire old memory of Israel. It makes its claim for Jesus, and it expects a response.

The response to the sermon is the exchange of vv. 37-41. It is clear that such preaching (then or now) is not simply a verbal or intellectual exercise. It requires a response. It anticipates a transformation. One must now take into account a new governance (wrought in Easter) and come to terms with it. One must decide afresh.

The sermon drives Peter's listeners to the urgent question: "What shall we do?" (v. 37). Clearly something must be done; it is not, however, clear *what* must be done. What indeed does the resurrection require? Peter's ready answer is not unlike the answer already given by John the Baptist (Luke 3:11-14): "Repent" (v. 38). Resurrection evokes repentance. A new governance requires a new obedience. Preaching the resurrection intends to destabilize old patterns of life and uproot every hearer from the presumed world in which we have grown comfortable. Contrary to popular, uncritical religion, repentance is not a moralistic requirement, but a comprehensive imperative that life must be reoriented in terms of foundational presuppositions, about power, about right, about what is good.

The sign of repentance and its initial act is baptism in the name of Jesus, for forgiveness. Peter's testimony thus is congruent with Jesus' own invitation (cf. Mark 1:15). The resurrection is an invitation to live in a world where forgiveness prevails for us, for all persons, for all of creation. For that reason, the church's creed in its last article has linked "the forgiveness of sins," and "the resurrection of the body." Both phrases are affirmations about the evangelical capacity to begin again. Indeed, Hannah Arendt has concluded that the most radical claim of the New Testament is not resurrection, but forgiveness. It is the power of the resurrection which permits forgiveness.

Out of these two imperatives, "Repent, be baptized," the text issues a promise: "You shall receive the gift of the Holy Spirit" (v. 38). Again, the subsequent creed of the church has understood and articulated the connection of these factors, for forgiveness and resurrection together are subsumed under, "I believe in the Holy Spirit." The Spirit must be given by God. It cannot be forced, preempted, or possessed. A great deal of misunderstanding pertains to "the Spirit," because of popular distortion. The "Holy Spirit" in this connection should be treated neither as a *theologumenon*, that is, as a "person" of God, nor as a marginal religious phenomenon evidenced in freakish religious behavior.

Rather "Holy Spirit" refers to God's root power to create new life. It is the wind that blows in creation to cause a genuine newness. In this act of repentance and baptism, when a person renounces other, *ersatz* sources of life, when a person breaks with fake definitions of reality and faces the sovereign power of the crucified one, the wind of God blows and creates, makes new, restores, and life begins again. The fruit of the Spirit, i.e., the evidence of being gifted by God's life-wind, is freedom for new life, courage in the face of old modes of life, power to heal and transform.

The promise of new life for believers through repentance and baptism is a remarkable extrapolation from the resurrection of Jesus. Now everything is focused on new life *for us*, new life which requires and permits a decisive break with other assumptions about and supports for life. In his response to the question of v. 37, Peter issues one other imperative which asserts the urgency of the new choice: "Be saved from this crooked generation" (v. 40). Peter anticipates a break with the death-oriented world around. The term "generation" here means species or genre. The main genre of humans is one of distortion. That distorted species is under judgment from God. The invitation to life new from the resurrection calls for disengagement from that genre, and from its deathly destiny.

Baptism, however, is not an escape. It is an embrace of newness. The early church clearly is not a withdrawn sect which immunized itself from public reality. Rather it was a force which participated in the public world at great risk, but with great power.

The "crooked generation" that is destined for trouble from God consists in those who live in fearful, brutal, oppressive ways. Because our reading is in Acts, it is legitimate to compare this response of Peter with the response of John in Luke 3:10-14. There the response urges listeners to disengage from injustice, exploitation, and violence. Here we are not given such a specific answer, but the same alternatives are no doubt intended.

The question posed by this conversation (vv. 37-41) is a demanding one for the North American church. Either we habitually ignore such imperatives, or we reduce them to private issues of "virtue." Neither disregard nor privatization is permitted by the text. Peter speaks about disengagement from the theological assumptions and fundamental policies of dominant society. The sermon is an invitation to have the congregation astonished, intimidated, and delighted that the truth of the resurrection does indeed authorize another way in the world, not coopted by the brutal deathliness and the demanding modes of life all around us.

Verses 41-47 characterize the new community which emerges from this preaching, which stands in stark contrast to "this crooked generation." Everything in these dazzling verses is authorized and empowered by the newly given life-wind of God. We may identify four aspects of this new life which flow from the resurrection:

1. This is a community *under simple, clear discipline* (v. 42). This community engaged in a study of the normative apostolic tradition which must be regularly reappropriated. It also practiced regularly the Eucharist, and in its prayer submitted its life to God's purpose.

2. This community was a trusting fellowship with an *alternative economic practice* (vv. 44-45). The members of this new community had no need for self-sufficiency and so could share. This is in contrast to the "crooked generation" which is under judgment because it refuses such vulnerability and pursues self-sufficiency.

3. This community is *powered for transformative action* (v. 43). It performed "many signs and wonders," i.e., acts of healing and rescue. There was freedom to commit overt acts of love, mercy, and justice which changed the world. Notice the phrase "signs and wonders" is the same phrase used for Jesus in v. 22. The church has power and freedom to do what Jesus did.

4. The community that so trusted the testimony is marked by *joyous, generative self-abandonment*, expressed as neighborliness and doxology (vv. 46-47). There is no more fear or defensiveness before God or humankind. This is a church unfettered, unafraid, and therefore empowered.

Who wouldn't want to live such a life? We resist if we prefer our membership in "this crooked generation." We may prefer to be

• without simple discipline,
• without alternative economics practice,
• without power for transformative actions,
• without joyous, generous self-abandonment.

We may not want to repent and be baptized. We may not believe the witnesses to the resurrection. We may not want the gift of the Spirit. Resistance is possible. The text, however, makes available a wondrous alternative, that leaves us stunned at who we could be . . . because Jesus is raised.

EPISTLE: 1 PETER 1:17-23

As the sermon of Peter invites people into the church, so the epistle of Peter urges the church to act on its faith. This passage strings together a rich sequence of phrases, any part of which offers a rich interpretive possibility. It may be most useful to explicate the logic of the passage under three themes:

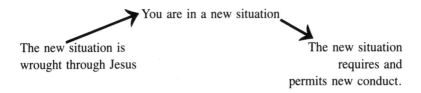

The new situation is wrought through Jesus

You are in a new situation

The new situation requires and permits new conduct.

The move is from christological affirmation to ecclesiological and ethical imperative.

1. Christians are placed in *a wholly new situation*. They are summoned to act differently because of the changed reality in which they live. We may identify three characterizations for this new situation. *(a)* You were *redeemed* from futile ways (v. 18). Jesus is the sacrifice offered which restores life to the baptized. Preransomed life has been marked as "darkness," "no people," "not receive mercy," that is, dominated by fear, alienation, and death (cf. 2:9-10). *(b)* You have been *born anew* through the word of God (v. 23). The imagery (cf. 2:2, John 3:3) suggests a contrast in being recreated for God's purpose by God's power. *(c)* You have *confidence in God* (v. 21). The believer need no longer rely on self or on powers that cannot keep their promises. The passage clearly strains to find language adequate for the unutterable newness given in the gospel.

2. That new situation is *wrought through Jesus* and is the will of God. The text stays close to the normative affirmation of crucifixion and resurrection. The crucifixion of Jesus is the subject of v. 19 (precious blood, lamb without blemish). The resurrection is explicit in v. 21. It is the resurrection that is the ground of faith and hope. Thus crucifixion leads to ransom, resurrection leads to faith and hope. The life of Jesus is decisive for the community of the baptized.

The new situation wrought through Jesus is rooted in God's abiding will. God destined Jesus' history before creation (v. 20). It is God's word that comes to visibility in Jesus. The new situation is as sure as God's own resolve.

3. The new situation *mandates new obedience*. The ethical expectation in vv. 13-16, just before our passage, invites the church to "set your hope on grace," "to be holy." Here it is "conduct yourself with fear," that is, with awareness of God's decisive purpose (v. 17). Then the text becomes quite specific: "Love one another earnestly from the heart" (v. 22). The text connects the abiding will of God and the specific conduct of the church. The conduct of the church is not a matter of casual option, but manifests the eternal intention of God.

The text reflects urgency in its summons. Perhaps the believers addressed were not as full of confidence as they are said to be (v. 21). Perhaps they are inclined to compromise. The most durable, reliable grounding for new life is the imperishable word of God that abides. Everything depends on God's promissory word that is enacted in Jesus. When proclaimed, received, and believed, that word is sufficient grounding and motivation for new life. Christians live differently, powered by God's abiding purpose.

GOSPEL: LUKE 24:13-35

(On vv. 13-35, see the exposition for "Easter Evening or Easter Monday.")

These texts, the originary narrative (Luke 24:13-35), the preaching of Peter (Acts 2:14a, 36-47), and the summons to obedience in the epistle (1 Peter 1:17-23), all focus on the church. The question raised in each case is, What will we do with the risen Jesus? How shall we respond? The answer, urged in these texts, is that an adequate response to the risen Jesus requires the formation of an alterative community that is committed to a different public practice of care. The eucharistic accent of the gospel, the promise of the Spirit, the commendation of an ethic of love, the explication of a new economics, the gift of power for new life—all testify to a community open to God's power for new life. That openness is made real and possible by a disengagement from all the ways of futility that block God's gift of life. Preaching from these texts invites the awesome conviction that such a new community is in every generation, including ours, a gift granted in the gospel.

The Fourth Sunday of Easter

Lutheran	Roman Catholic	Episcopal	Common Lectionary
Acts 6:1–9, 7:2a, 51–60	Acts 2:14a, 36–41	Acts 6:1–9, 7:2a, 51–60	Acts 2:42–47
1 Pet. 2:19–25	1 Pet. 2:20–25	1 Pet. 2:19–25	1 Pet. 2:19–25
John 10:1–10	John 10:1–10	John 10:1–10	John 10:1–10

The early church lived an endangered life. It lived under and was summoned by startling newness, the new rule of the risen Christ. That startling news of Jesus put the church in profound tension with all that was old and settled. That tension created a threat to the church, for the power of all that was old wanted to stop, silence, and destroy the newness unleashed in the resurrection.

GOSPEL: JOHN 10:1-10

The Fourth Gospel presents a sharp contrast between Jesus and all the religious alternatives prior to him: the "good wine" and "poor wine" (2:1-11), the old birth and new birth (3:1-11), the old worship and the new worship (4:21). In this text, a like contrast is present through the shepherd metaphor. All other would-be shepherds are false and do damage to the sheep, while Jesus is the true shepherd.

In vv. 1-6 the contrast is total. Two options are offered (vv. 1-2): The thief and robber enter the sheepfold surreptitiously, that is, without legitimacy, while the true shepherd enters properly, as he has a right to do. The true shepherd knows the sheep and values them by name (vv. 3-4). As the shepherd knows their names, so the sheep know his voice. There is recognition, trust, and bonding between shepherd and sheep. Both parties fulfill their role. The shepherd wisely leads, the sheep trustingly follow. By contrast, the "stranger" who enters falsely is not well received. The sheep do not know his voice and will not follow him (v. 5). The two possible shepherds are characterized, but no identification is made. The narrative asserts what is surely known in a pastoral economy about the bonding of shepherd and sheep, but the metaphor is too dense for Jesus' listeners (v. 6).

In vv. 7-18, the empty metaphor of vv. 1-6 is given historical, christological specificity. Now Jesus enters the metaphorical scenario. The words
move from "the shepherd" to "I" (v. 7). The countershepherd has come
to do damage to the sheep and will exploit them.

The positive alternative to v. 8 in vv. 7 and 9, however, does not handle
the metaphor consistently. In these verses, Jesus is not shepherd but the
door of the sheepfold (cf. v. 3). In this changed image, we are given not
a shepherd who leads, but entry to the fold where the sheep will be safe,
protected, and secure. Thus Jesus is the access point to safety and well-
being. The figure of the door acknowledges that the sheep are endangered,
exposed not only to the abuse of false shepherds, but attacks of wild beasts
(v. 12). The sheep are in jeopardy and kept safely only when they enter
(through Jesus) to the well-protected enclosure.

In v. 10, the contrast of vv. 1-2 is reiterated. Now we are told explicitly
what the thief will do: steal, kill, destroy. Jesus is the alternative shepherd
who gives abundant life (i.e., food, water, safe well-being). Thus the
contrast is complete. The thief endangers the sheep, Jesus cares for the
sheep and enhances their life. It is only with the good shepherd that the
sheep can prosper.

Two factors make the metaphorical articulation of the narrative difficult.
First, there is inconsistency and instability in the metaphor. Jesus is variously the door and the shepherd. The "stranger" is variously thief, robber,
hireling, sometimes exploiting the sheep, sometimes abandoning them.
Second, the narrative is clear about the activity of Jesus, but gives no hint
of the meaning of the countermetaphor or the identity of the "stranger."
We may imagine the "stranger" is any counterclaim to Jesus. In the Fourth
Gospel the "stranger" is plausibly the older claim of Judaism. The accent,
however, is not on the negative. Rather the central point is the utter self-
giving of Jesus who makes the vulnerable flock utterly safe. This flock
hears his voice, trusts his presence, relies on his protection, and lives by
his self-giving. The metaphor asserts the only safety available to a community at risk. The church trustingly relies on Jesus for its well-being.
Every alternative jeopardizes.

EPISTLE: 1 PETER 2:19-25

The epistle is a meditation on the vulnerability of the church in a society
where it lacks conventional social supports. The life and witness of the
church place it in continuing jeopardy. It lives as a community of outsiders.
Its presence is unwelcome in the world. Its witness evokes hostility. In

such a situation of risk, Christians may wonder why such a destiny is required and whether it is worth it. Those who suffer for their faith are not unaware that there are safer ways to live, with faith less urgent, a witness less offensive. Our text occurs in a list of admonitions, urging Christians to be content in their subordinate positions (v. 18). When the text is drawn into the lectionary configuration where we have it, we may notice fresh accents. This is a text urging Christians to endure suffering that belongs to the vocation of their faith.

The community of faith must suffer (vv. 19-20). Christians suffer *because* they are faithful. They suffer for faith, and may have confidence that their suffering is appropriate to and approved by God. They do not need to ask in wonderment if their suffering bespeaks something amiss. They are approved by God in their suffering and so can bear the pain. Suffering derived from obedience (vv. 19, 21) is contrasted with suffering that is punishment for wrongdoing (v. 20). The "right suffering" here enjoined is that which is willingly embraced in faith and inevitable in a faithful life that evokes social hostility.

Verse 21 provides an explicit link between the suffering of the church and the suffering of Jesus (cf. Matt. 5:10-12). The rightness of the church's suffering is rooted in the fact that Jesus suffered. It was Jesus' daring obedience, in conflict with established authority, that caused his suffering. He is model and example for the church whose call is to the same suffering for the same obedience.

Verses 22-24 pursue the christological rootage in detail. Jesus' suffering is a model for the church. He suffered innocently (v. 22). He did not respond in kind to those who brutalized him (v. 23). He had confidence in a "just judgment"; that is, he trusted in a much larger reckoning which would override the particularities of his unjust treatment. Jesus suffered innocently and willingly, as the church also is to respond to suffering (vv. 22-23). He is example and model. In v. 24, however, a major shift is made. Jesus' suffering is salvific! His suffering mediates life to others, permitting others to lead a changed existence. Jesus is not only model (v. 21), but also power and authorization for healing (cf. Isa. 53:4-5).

Verse 25 provides a powerful link to the Gospel reading. Here there is no false shepherd, only straying sheep who are exceedingly exposed and vulnerable. Now the faithful flock has acknowledged the rightful shepherd. They know his voice and submit to his protection. It is Jesus who will keep the believing community utterly safe, guard their lives, and keep their persons.

The language of this unit is disconcertingly open-ended. Nothing is specified about why the church suffers. The subject may be specific persecution, or simply social standing as slaves. The epistle reading recognizes that suffering belongs to the enduring, almost definitional character of the church. In its very being, the church is a scandal in the world, embodying a scandalous alternative, exiled from accepted norms of conduct (1:1), summoned to a different obedience, shaped by a different loyalty. The linkage between the issues of church behavior (vv. 18-20), and the power of Christ (vv. 21-25) is crucial for proclaiming this text when the church is culturally co-opted. It is because Jesus is an oddity that the church is characterized as odd. The sheep follow him in attitude and in action. Therefore the church can be no less odd, scandalous, and affrontive than is Jesus. The interpretive point is to ask how, where, and in what ways the "flock" in this generation is to be at risk and vulnerable. A church not at risk and vulnerable is not reflective of nor trustful of the suffering One who heals and authorizes. Moreover, such a flock knows little of the massive assurance of the shepherd who guards our lives.

FIRST LESSON: ACTS 6:1-9, 7:2a, 51-60

Abruptly, Stephen appears in the midst of the church. In these two chapters he appears, performs dramatically, and is eliminated. That is all there is to him. In that brief appearance, however, Stephen enacts what is most crucial and powerful in the Christian life. He embodies the risk and vulnerability which both the Gospel and epistle lessons have voiced.

The presenting problem of the early church is quite practical. Daily administrative details in the life of the church were not adequately handled (6:2). A new group of persons is chosen for diaconal work, duly authorized by prayer and the laying on of hands (6:3-6). Stephen is among them.

The narrative memory of the church cannot restrain itself about Stephen. He is among those who are "of good repute, full of the Spirit and wisdom" (6:3). He is singled out, however, from the other six chosen. He is a "man full of faith and of the Holy Spirit" (6:5), "full of grace and power," who did "signs and wonders" (6:8). Indeed, his face is "like the face of an angel" (6:15). Stephen is among the most powerful, effective, attractive, irresistible embodiments of Christian life and faith that we will meet.

There is, nevertheless, an oddity about Stephen's work. He is authorized to "serve tables" (6:2). Probably this is not as menial as the task sounds to us. He is to direct the daily distribution of food and to be sure the resources of the community are managed equitably on behalf of the disadvantaged. Our opening verses suggest there was an important controversy about resource management: a dispute about power and privilege. Stephen's commission concerns resource management.

The narrative, however, presents Stephen in a very different role, filled with power and courage, as preacher, teacher, witness, and interpreter of the dangerous claims of the gospel. The adversaries of the church confront him (6:9); they cannot withstand his eloquence and power (6:10). He preaches and evokes a response of hostility (6:11). His sermon ranges over the entire memory of Israel, until finally he draws his listeners in at the last episode in that long recital. According to Stephen, "You always resist the Spirit" (7:51). Stephen, by contrast is "full of the Holy Spirit" (6:5). Thus the dispute is not about the history of Israel. It is about the dangerous power of the Holy Spirit in the community of the faithful.

Stephen and his opponents are models of resistance to and reception of the Spirit. "Resistance to the Spirit" has caused the killing of the prophets, the silencing of those voices who spoke of God's future (7:52). In contrast to such resistance, Stephen, filled with the very power the others resist, bears witness to the ongoing rule of Christ (7:55). He reports a vision of Jesus in power at God's throne (7:56). His listeners are affected, because they are scandalized that the crucified one could be the one who governed. The crucified one is a scandal and a stumbling block, for Jesus' suffering love is vindicated as the way of real power in the world. In that daring affirmation, Stephen delegitimates all other forms of power, subverts all other claims to authority, nullifies all their interpretations of history, overrides all other narrative promises. His preaching dismantles every other perception of reality, in an awesome claim for the rule of King Jesus in heaven and on earth.

No wonder Stephen evoked such hostility! His daring rhetoric brought an end to the trusted world of his listeners. Their response is immediate and passionate. They cried out (v. 57). They stopped their ears. They rushed upon him. They cast him out. They stoned him. Stephen dies brutalized and undefended.

The narrator, however, tells us of the astonishing character of his death. He died a free man, unencumbered by fear or hate. He died in imitation of Jesus (v. 60; cf. 1 Peter 2:21). As Stephen died, he said two things: "Receive my spirit," echoing the prayer of Jesus (cf. Luke 23:46). He then said, "Do not hold this against them," echoing the petition of Jesus (Luke 23:34). He died as he had lived, following the example of Jesus. He died full of power, freedom, and courage, so filled with God's future that he was a threat to those who heard him. He is the church's first martyr.

Such a descriptive verdict, however, should not lead us away from the dramatic reality of *resisting* and *receiving* the Spirit. Stephen embodies the church's best posture of fidelity. He is vulnerable and exposed, "approved" of God.

This narrative from Acts seems to stand in tension with the promise of the Gospel and the epistle. The Gospel promises the faithful they "will be saved," to "go in and out and find pasture . . . have life and have it abundantly" (vv. 9-10). The epistle witnesses to the "shepherd and guardian of your souls" (v. 5). Stephen, however, died a violent death. This seeming incongruity, between promised care and violent death, however, is characteristic of the church's faith and experience. The narrative in Acts asserts that Stephen did indeed have the abundant life and did have his soul kept and guarded. Stephen stands as a witness that a life of serious faith is not to be assessed by the norms of the world. His is a life in a very different dimension, ready for risk, powered by resurrection, filled with the Spirit. Stephen embodies and enacts the faith and assurance of the other two readings.

ALTERNATIVE FIRST LESSON: ACTS 2:42-47

This reading is explicated among the texts for The Third Sunday of Easter.

The Fifth Sunday of Easter

Lutheran	Roman Catholic	Episcopal	Common Lectionary
Acts 17:1–15	Acts 6:1–7	Acts 17:1–15	Acts 7:55–60
1 Pet. 2:4–10	1 Pet. 2:4–9	1 Pet. 2:1–10	1 Pet. 2:2–10
John 14:1–12	John 14:1–12	John 14:1–14	John 14:1–14

FIRST LESSON: ACTS 17:1-15

This reading locates Paul and Silas in two preaching confrontations, Thessalonica (vv. 1-9) and Beroea (vv. 10-14). Their preaching receives contrasting responses of rejection and acceptance.

In Thessalonica (vv. 1-9), Paul joins issues with practicing Jews to argue from Scripture that Jesus is the one to whom the Scriptures (the Old Testament) witnesses (vv. 2-3). The early church insists that the Christian gospel complements the anticipations of the Old Testament. The long expected "Christ" is indeed Jesus!

Some who heard Paul were persuaded. They include "many" Greeks and "not a few" women (v. 4). The narrative, however, is not interested in them. Interest focuses on those who resist the interpretive match between old promises and Christian claims. The accused Christians are enmeshed with disturbed authorities and are released only after posting bond (v. 9).

The dramatic center of this episode is in vv. 6-7 where the charges are stated against Christian preaching. Of special interest is the fact that the resistance of the Thessalonicans is ill-joined to the affirmations of Paul and Silas. Paul's preaching is an *interpretive religious* claim linking Jesus to the old tradition (vv. 2-3). The accusation, however, is a *sociopolitical one: (a)* they have "turned the world upside down," and *(b)* they have acted against Roman authority in their claim for Jesus as king (vv. 6-7). The shift from interpretive religious claim to sociopolitical charge is a dramatic and telling move. It is not a dishonest or gratuitous move.

Indeed, Paul's detractors faithfully construe Paul's preaching and shrewdly discern its "worldly implications." They understand that the religious claims of vv. 2-3 have deep and dangerous social implications. This risen Jesus is indeed the awaited Messiah; this new reality shatters all conventional categories for understanding old reality. Jesus is indeed "another king" (v. 7). All other authority (including Rome) is destabilized and delegitimated. There is no compromise or accommodation between the new reality of Jesus and the old arrangements of world power and world order. Opposition in Thessalonica is not evoked by an esoteric interpretive dispute. It is rightly evoked by an urge to keep the world unchanged, to hold things as they were. To keep the world "wrong side up" (as it now is) requires rejection of the gospel.

The second preaching situation, the synagogue at Beroea, forms a sharp and welcome contrast to that of Thessalonica (vv. 10-15). Many believed (v. 12), Paul and Silas were well received, and their gospel was accepted. Surprisingly, the narrative suggests that the more favorable reception is because of "higher class" people, that is, they were "more noble" (v. 11). The responding people were not "pushovers." An argument had to be made on behalf of the gospel. The listeners at Beroea do not perceive the gospel as treason against Caesar, as charged at Thessalonica.

The happy reception at Beroea is, however, interrupted by the hostile Thessalonians (v. 13). The troublemakers from Thessalonica intervene in Beroea. Quickly Paul departs from the trouble (v. 14).

The text makes clear that the gospel evokes different, powerful responses. The preaching of the gospel places people in crisis and requires a decision. It is a decision concerning Jesus, the resurrection, the messiah, and the meaning of Scripture. It is also a decision about the world, about Caesar and power, and about the right shape of the world. *Gospel* and *world* are inextricably joined together. The gospel shows the world's distortedness and corrects it. Resistance to the gospel and its preaching may be evoked by a desire to keep the world distorted. A decision about the gospel is in every case a decision about the world. Where preaching does not call the world into crisis, it likely is not faithful about Jesus.

EPISTLE: 1 PETER 2:1-10

The text from Acts is an account of persons just as they come to faith. The epistle reading is addressed to "you who believe" (v. 7). It is an appeal that believers should embrace, affirm, embody, and act out the faith they profess. The text is organized into an initial appeal (vv. 1-3), a collage of Old Testament texts that point to Jesus (vv. 4-8), and an assertion of the church's peculiar identity (vv. 9-10). The text is addressed to those who seem lax about their faith and are unsure of their grounding.

The *initial appeal* is stated in two imperatives (vv. 1-3). The first, negative imperative summons the community away from destructive behavior: "put away" (v. 1). The language is that of a baptismal formula, calling the believers to desist from action inappropriate to faith. The second, positive imperative is stated in a metaphor of nourishing food given by the gospel (vv. 2-3): *(a)* believers are to yearn for pure spiritual milk, that is, the simple, uncontaminated nourishment of the gospel; *(b)* this milk should stimulate growth and maturation in the gospel; *(c)* the imperative "long for" is supported by a first taste, anticipating that this taste will be satisfying and compelling. There are three terms in the metaphor: milk, grow up, and taste. All present the image of a newborn baby who is well-fed, satisfied, and growing—a picture of health. The substantive terms of the appeal are also threefold, spiritual, salvation, kindness. This rich and inviting metaphor promises satisfaction that will "wean" the believer away from false nourishment, which is expressed as "malice, guile, insincerity, envy, and slander" (v. 1).

A collage of Old Testament texts points to Jesus as the grounding for this new life (vv. 4-8). Verses 4-5 use the metaphor of "stone" to link

Christ and church. Jesus, who has been rejected by the world and valued by God, is the center and focus of a new life (v. 4). As Jesus is a "living stone," so Christians are living stones who are built around the cornerstone to be an edifice for Christ's use (v. 5).

After the brief departure from the metaphor in v. 5, the text returns in vv. 6-8 to the governing metaphor of stone. In a quote from Isa. 28:16, v. 6 speaks of a cornerstone, chosen and precious to God. This allusion to Jesus is an invitation to accept Jesus as the center of the new edifice of faith. The text has a difficult time staying with the metaphor, because the figure of stone seems not capable of containing the rich play of images affirmed. While v. 6 states the positive possibility of a faith that is a treasure, vv. 7-8 are aware of a rejection of the stone (cf. Ps. 118:22) that causes stumbling, and tripping over the discarded stone. As believing is a positive response to the stone, so disobeying is a way of rejecting which leads to stumbling (v. 8). The metaphor, used with considerable imagination, is articulated to urge that the church stay very close to Jesus. The mixed metaphor speaks on the one hand of stones organized around a cornerstone. On the other hand, it speaks of believing in, disobeying, and rejecting. This rather unstable and incongruent set of figures affirms that it is the character and purpose of Jesus that shapes the life of the church. The church derives from Jesus.

The allusion to a negative destiny in v. 8 prepares for the dramatic construct of v. 9: *But you!* The "you" is not named. It is the same "you" of direct address in the imperatives of vv. 2, 4, the direct address of v. 2, and the pronouns of vv. 3, 5. 7. The text concerns you the church, you the beloved of God, you the community created for faith and obedience.

Verses 9-10 contain one of the most treasured and dramatic characterizations of the church in the New Testament. The language, like most of vv. 6-8, is saturated with Old Testament references (cf. Exod. 19:5-6 and Hos. 2:23). The language of ancient Israel is now adapted for the church. The church is to be an utterly new people formed out of God's purpose to have a mediating office in the world, making possible healing contact between God and the world (v. 9). Through an act of enormous love, the disobedient community is reclaimed to be God's beloved faithful people. The Mosaic assertion (v. 9) and the poetry of Hosea (v. 10) assert that this community has no right to be, but God has loved and reloved this community into existence. The church exists because of God's unconditional, unqualified, community-creating love.

The concrete ethics of vv. 1-3 and the superlative theological grounding of vv. 9-10 are held together by the claims of Christ in vv. 4-8, and by the affirmation of the church's faith. The church is called to live differently in the world, chosen, royal, holy, and God's own people, rooted in God's powerful will and God's profound mercy.

The summons Paul issues to his listeners in Thessalonica and Beroea is the affirmation given here by Peter. The church community is no casual, careless, or incidental gathering of people. It is a special community, rooted in different realities and summoned to different conduct. Belief is an active decision to be peculiar in the world. The intense rhetoric of this text is not very different from the threat of "turning the world upside down."

GOSPEL: JOHN 14:1-14

In this text, Jesus prepares the church for its life in his absence. In the place of "presence," Jesus urges the church to "believe" during the absence (v. 1). The belief here urged anticipates Erik Erikson's initial stage of human development, "basic trust"; that is, confidence in the reality, fidelity, and significance of Jesus even when Jesus is not physically, visibly present.

The text moves in four rhetorical units. First, Jesus urges trust in God and in himself with the assurance that there is a "place prepared" for the community of faith (vv. 1-4). The language is impressionistic and lacking in concrete reference. While our conventional funeral sermons treat the place as "heaven," it is more likely that the language of "place" is used for a relationship (cf. 4:20-21). That is, the absence of Jesus is not permanent. Jesus leaves, yet he "abides." In Jesus' returning to be with the church, the church will be in Jesus' presence (v. 3). Jesus' departure is not an act of infidelity; his coming and going are acts of solidarity. The relation of Jesus and church is not static or one-dimensional. It is, however, a relation requiring profound faithfulness, in presence and in absence. The text invites the church utterly to be "at home," in the midst of a situation in which all absence, alienation, and dislocation are overcome. Moreover, the way to be "at home" is already known. The way is the way of Jesus, a way of trust and obedience. The early church had learned that the journey with Jesus is indeed the home with the Father. Thus Nelle Morton can say, *The Journey Is Home* (Boston: Beacon Press, 1985).

Second, the question of Thomas permits Jesus to be more explicit (vv. 5-7). Thomas is the disciples' voice of honest bewilderment and uncertainty. Jesus' statement is inscrutable. His language of place and of way, of journey and destination, is profoundly metaphorical and elusive. It requires interpretation that only Jesus can give. In his response to Thomas, Jesus moves abruptly from the language of place and journey to speak directly about relations to himself and to the hidden God whom he calls "Father" (vv. 6-7).

Jesus is the way, the route, the journey; Jesus's life, teaching, mission, and presence are what the church is to practice, a way of mission and servanthood. Jesus as the way leads to the goal who is the Father. Thus the language of place and way is transposed into language of relation. The place or the goal is the Father. The route to the Father is Jesus.

Jesus' language refers to the hidden one, who is holy and inscrutable, who is present decisively and distinctively in the life of Jesus. What matters is the unique intimacy of the "place" and the "way," God and Jesus.

The exclusive claim that Jesus is the only route to God is a problematic claim. This verse has been endlessly troublesome in the life of the church, for it articulates a claim for Christianity that has bred triumphalism and invited totalitarianism in the service of the institutional church. It must be recognized that this claim is not the whole of the New Testament witness. The exclusive claim here is not an attack on other ways, but is indeed an assurance to the disciples. Life with Jesus, in his way, is the known, accepted, celebrated, assured way to our ultimate "place" of well-being. The church must indeed come to terms with Jesus and can indeed count on Jesus.

By the third element of the text, the discussion with Philip, the metaphor of place and way is now abandoned (vv. 8-11). The discussion clearly concerns the relation of Jesus and God, the revealer and the revealed. The disciples want to "see" God, want to enter the holy of holies, want privileged access to the hidden one where no one is given access (v. 8; cf. Exod. 33:18-23). Jesus' answer is both assurance and limit (vv. 9-11).

The text does not linger long over the hiddenness of the "Father." It focuses rather on the visibility, accessibility, and "knownness" of Jesus. What counts is the one known. That is enough for Philip and for the church! Moreover, the one known is known through "the works themselves," the works of Jesus. Such is the intimacy of father and son, of journey and goal, that the works of Jesus are in fact done by the Father. "The works" are healing transformation wrought by Jesus. The Father is known through a blind boy healed (9:25), a crowd fed (6:11-14), a dead man raised (11:44). There is no escape from concreteness into "metaphysics."

Finally, as if to stress the accent of "works," we move from "the works of the Father" to the works "you will do" (vv. 12-14). Theological talk eventuates in missional activity. What began with worry about the departure of Jesus (v. 4) is now talk about the gift of power in the life of the church for the work the church is to do. The church is to do what Jesus has done, which is what God does. When the church does its obedient work, it knows "I will do it" (v. 14). It is through the dailiness of church obedience that the hidden Father is glorified!

ALTERNATIVE FIRST LESSON: ACTS 7:55-60

Acts 7:55-60 has been discussed in The Fourth Sunday of Easter.

The Sixth Sunday of Easter

Lutheran	Roman Catholic	Episcopal	Common Lectionary
Acts 17:22–31	Acts 8:5–8, 14–17	Acts 17:22–31	Acts 17:22–31
1 Pet. 3:15–22	1 Pet. 3:15–18	1 Pet. 3:8–18	1 Pet. 3:13–22
John 14:15–21	John 14:15–21	John 15:1–8	John 14:15–21

GOSPEL: JOHN 14:15-21

The disciples, who are addressed by Jesus, are utterly unlike the world. The disciples live under a different command, are given a different spirit, serve a different God, and engage in a different love. This instruction of Jesus, anticipating his departure and absence, asserts how the church is to order its life and practice its faith during Jesus' absence.

The church must respond to and can rely upon God's sovereignty. That sovereignty is known in command and as Paraclete (vv. 15-17). The church is under command; it loves God through its obedience (v. 15). The community-defining command, however, is new and unexpected. It is not a command to enhance or benefit God, but to love each other, in suffering, self-giving ways. The command is connected to the power of truth, an active force which gives life and overcomes all the fraudulence that leads to death (v. 17). The command is an invitation to live a different life together, unlike the ways of the world. The gift of God's Spirit is assurance that God's own self will continue to be active and powerful in the community (v. 16-17). Unlike the world, this community hosts powerful truth and enacts transformative love.

This text responds to the church's sense of abandonment. Jesus is about to depart. That departure, however, does not equal abandonment. The church ostensibly is "orphaned" (*orphanous*, i.e., desolate, v. 18). The church is in fact not orphaned. The church is cared for even when it imagines otherwise. The continued care of God for the church is articulated in two different ways. First, the Spirit is given who will abide (vv. 16-17). Proto-trinitarian language is used to speak of the Spirit's presence when Jesus is absent. Then a second assurance is given (v. 18-23). It is expressed in apocalyptic language, with such formulae as "yet a little while" and "in that day." There is a brief absence and a soon-to-happen return of Jesus to be in the midst of the church.

There seems no obvious way to reconcile the language of "indwelling spirit" and "returning Christ," for two different images are used. It is possible that the two phrases together indicate uncertainty and disagreement in the church concerning its future with God. For our purposes, it is sufficient to recognize that the church used various modes of language to witness to its central conviction: The church is not alone and will not be alone!

The apocalyptic language of assured companionship in the future, "in a little while," is presented under three rubrics: *(a)* "I will come to you" (v. 18); this is a hope for Jesus' return; *(b)* you "will be loved by my father" (v. 21); and *(c)* "We will come to him and make our home with him" (v. 23). The language lacks precision; it is, however, passionate in its main claim. The main resource of the church is the enduring love, power, and presence of God. In some preaching, as in the book of Acts, the resurrection of Jesus bespeaks a deep break with all that is old. This text, however, focuses on the continuity wrought by God's love and faithfulness. Even Jesus' departure does not disrupt God's sustained attentiveness to the church.

The answer to Judas indicates that the promised presence is not some general ontological affirmation about God in the world (v. 22). God's promised presence peculiarly concerns the church, the faithful community of the commandment. Thus the world cannot receive the Spirit (v. 17). Jesus will not be manifested to the world (vv. 22-23). "The world" consists in all those who do not know the Father, who do not obey the command, who do not host the Spirit of truth, who do not love Jesus. This text, however, is not addressed to the world, and is not interested in castigating the world.

The world is mentioned only to establish the contrast. Affirmations about the love of the Father, the manifestation of the Son, and the gift of the Spirit are the core of the text. God in God's fullness is present to the faithful. That core assurance is bounded at the beginning and end of the text by love: "If you love . . . He who does not love" (vv. 15, 24). Everything depends on love. The capacity to love and the command to love are enduring. The practice of love makes the church staggeringly unlike the world. The text invites the church, now as then, to take note of its peculiar character and mandate.

EPISTLE: 1 PETER 3:13-22

Christians are to do what is right (v. 13). No specific content is given to this expectation. The writer assumes that the content of such conduct is already known in the church. Such conduct is not always well received and may lead to suffering (v. 14). Christians, however, have a grounding in their loyalty to Christ that authorizes and mandates such conduct, even when it is disapproved.

The language of vv. 15-17 makes clear that the recommended conduct is not universally accepted, "virtuous" activity. Christians are on trial, called to account in a hostile context for their action. They must make a "defense" *(apologia)*, not of their action, but of their hope. The articulation of hope, when done with good grace, will rout the critics (v. 16).

The linkage between doing *right* and having *hope* is crucial for the church at risk. It is that connection which prevents this text from being a mere moral urging. Christians are indeed urged to do right, but their action is grounded in and powered by their hope, "a living hope" rooted in Jesus' resurrection (cf. 1:3). This hope testifies that the power of life will finally prevail in the world. The substance of hope concerns the victory of God's power for life. We may imagine that the "right" Christians do is to witness to and enact that power for life in a world that is arranged in deathly ways. It is hope that makes Christians problematic in their transformative living and difficult to domesticate.

The "eccentric" behavior of Christians is rooted in the reality of Christ (vv. 18-20). Christ is to be reverenced (v. 15). Indeed, the action commended is "good behavior in Christ" (v. 16). As Christians are powered by the reality of Christ, so they are also to act out in their lives the reality of Christ. Thus in v. 18 the admonition moves to a christological reflection.

Now, we have no admonition but a highly stylized account of what Christ has wrought, which impinges upon, guides, authorizes, and empowers the conduct of the church.

These three verses are a powerful but odd convergence of themes (vv. 18-20). The overriding thesis is that the righteousness of Christ rescues even the unrighteous. It is Jesus' suffering and death that permits his obedience to save others, to bring the alienated into communion with God, to bring life to those who are dead. Verse 18 is a powerful, freighted summary of evangelical faith. The righteousness of Christ saves; derivatively, the righteousness of the Christian life is a powerful witness in the world.

The thesis of righteousness rescuing the unrighteous is stated in the most extreme form in v. 19. Jesus brought the gospel into the "citadel of evil," into the place of sovereign deathliness. There Jesus confronted the core power of wickedness and worked a rescue. There is no use or need to probe this verse ontologically. It is sufficient to discern its rhetorical intention. There is no place where Christ's saving righteousness is not powerful and efficacious. Think of the worst power of sin, evil, and death, and you think of a place where Christ will prevail and rescue!

The contrast of "righteous/unrighteous" is then exposited in terms of Noah, the flood, and God's patience (v. 20). In that drama, Noah is the righteous one, and the others are wicked (cf. Gen. 6:5-9). The memory of Noah, however, functions only as a type, for in fact, Christ is contrasted with Noah. Noah's saving power is limited to his immediate family (eight persons), beyond which all others were lost. By contrast, Christ saves even the wicked who are locked into the power of death.

The theme turns again in vv. 21-22. The reference to Noah, water, and saving in v. 20 leads, for this passionate writer, to baptism (v. 21). It is the sacramental act of water in the church that saves, as the ark saved Noah, as Christ's righteousness saves. Verse 21 invites us to a fresh and evangelical understanding of baptism. The sacrament has heretofore been understood as a cleansing. Now it is presented as an appeal for a clear conscience. That is, it is an invitation and summons to embrace goodness. Baptism is done by and for the righteous who intend obedience. These are qualified to appeal to God through the resurrection of Jesus. While baptism is the human access point, it is the power of the resurrection that is the power to save. The text ends in a doxology to the risen one who is sovereign (v. 22).

This text is complex and seems to proceed by an undisciplined association of ideas: do right → Christ's righteousness → saving → Noah → water → baptism → resurrection → sovereignty. The text makes an odd but passionate connection between *daring Christian obedience* and *resurrection faith*. Goodness in the world and the sovereignty of Christ over the world are linked together. The text is strangely congruous with John 14:1-14 in which abiding fidelity leads to "greater works." As in all these texts, the power of new life in Jesus permits genuinely new life by believers in the world.

FIRST LESSON: ACTS 17:22-31

Paul, the preacher to the nations, witnesses to the gospel in gentile territory. He frames his argument in the categories of Hellenistic philosophy and poetry (v. 28). Paul demonstrates how the gospel provides the clue even to pagan attempts at religion. This text might be useful for discerning and addressing our own cultural-religious situation:

1. There is a broad attempt at generic religion in Athens, as among us (vv. 22-23a). The "men of Athens" are "very religious," but their religion lacks identity and substance. Like Athens, our society is also filled with generic religion, a deep craving, a powerful yearning, and an unresolved restlessness.

2. The Christian apostle names the unnamed and knows the unknown (vv. 23b-29). Paul makes a sweeping, theonomous claim. He does much more than to mouth back to Athens its large, vague religious sensitivities. Indeed, he makes a characteristically Jewish argument about the generic sovereignty of God (whose name he still does not utter). He argues that God is the creator, a "self-starter," an agent with power to cause to be that which does not exist (vv. 24-25). The argument begins in doxology to the creator, containing a polemic, as this God is contrasted with the gods of the nations who are no gods at all. Unlike the other gods who are "no-gods," this God is free of localization, is the maker but is unmade by human hands, not needful but able to give life.

This creator God intends human creatures to people and share the earth (v. 26), to seek and serve God (v. 27), and to be God's "offspring" (v. 28). Paul quotes "your poets," that is, the classic Greek artists, but utilizes Hellenistic religion and art as a vehicle of his assertion of the Christian gospel. These verses assert the sovereign reality of God who gives life. Paul dismisses every Feuerbachian argument, and asserts God to be in reality God. Paul credits his Greek listeners with an inchoate sense of the true God, but it is only Paul who can name the object of their yearning.

3. Only in vv. 30-31 does Paul come to the point. Everything about God

summons humanity to repent, to come to a new loyalty to God. The world must turn to God because "by a man" the world will be judged. Paul has withheld his crucial reference until now. The man on whom everything hinges is Jesus. Notice that in the entire textual unit, "the man" is never named. Nonetheless, in context the name is clear. Jesus' authority is evidenced in his resurrection. "This man" will judge the whole world according to God's intention for the creation.

Paul does indeed name the unnamed God. That God is known "by a man." The sovereignty of God is known in and through the resurrection of Jesus. Humanity, including the men of Athens who prefer generic religion, must deal with the resurrection of Jesus and all that the Easter miracle asserts about God's reality and purpose, about humanity, about the world, and about faith. "That man" has been given new life by the same God who creates the world and who warrants loyalty by all humanity. The unnamed God is named, not by an appeal to metaphysics or philosophy, but by reference to Easter.

This text, like the Gospel and the epistle readings, has its primary focus on the centrality of Christ. In the Gospel reading it is Jesus' works which disclose God (John 14:11). In the epistle, it is the righteousness of Jesus that saves (1 Peter 3:18). Now it is "this man" who will judge. This Jesus, raised and ruling, is the new fact that the church celebrates and that the world must face. The risen Jesus is the embodiment of new power for life in the world.

The Ascension of Our Lord

Lutheran	Roman Catholic	Episcopal	Common Lectionary
Acts 1:1–11	Acts 1:1–11	Acts 1:1–11	Acts 1:1–11
Eph. 1:16–23	Eph. 1:17–23	Eph. 1:15–23	Eph. 1:15–23
Luke 24:44–53	Matt. 28:16–20	Luke 24:49–53	Luke 24:46–53 *or* Mark 16:9–16, 19–20

GOSPEL: LUKE 24:44-53

This reading consists in two parts, a word from Jesus (vv. 44-49), and a narrative closure (vv. 50-53). The words of Jesus voice the most crucial

accents of the faith of the church (vv. 44-49). Luke concludes his Gospel
with a faith summary that is to sustain the church in its larger mission,
depicted in the book of Acts. The claim made by Jesus is that his whole
life is a fulfillment of Scripture (v. 44). The Old Testament witnesses to
his passion and resurrection (vv. 46-47). This theological claim has par-
ticular reference to Hos. 6:2, but more broadly it asserts that all the promises
and claims of the Old Testament come to fruition in Jesus.

The christological claim (v. 46) is immediately tilted toward a missional
expectation (v. 47). The death and resurrection of Jesus serve to evoke
repentance and forgiveness. The events of Jesus' life are now transformative
events "to be preached in his name" to all nations (v. 47). The move from
Christology to church mission in these two verses prepares us for the church
narrative to follow in the book of Acts.

The mission that is rooted in Jesus is the mission entrusted to the church.
The church consists in witnesses (v. 48). The term "witness" moves in
two directions. It moves backward to the events around Jesus, his crucifixion and resurrection. The witnesses are the ones who have been present
and experienced those events. The term also moves forward. The witnesses
are the ones who will give testimony to others, and make available the
events of Jesus to those who could not themselves be present for the
originary experience. The witnesses are the ones who can transmit the
news of repentance and forgiveness to others, so that all the nations can
begin again in faith and forgiveness.

The vocation of giving such testimony is demanding and risky. It cannot
be undertaken simply as a matter of firm resolve. It demands a grant of
power "from on high" (v. 49). It is this power that is now promised,
authorization given by God to embody and enact the news of the gospel.

Luke's narrative closure is terse (vv. 50-53). Jesus "parted." That is all.
He was gone. As he left, he blessed them. The response of the disciples
to this parting is worth noting. Whereas in the Fourth Gospel, there is
great anxiety about the departure of Jesus, here there is great joy (v. 52).
There is great joy because the disciples trust the promise of power to be
given. Moreover, Luke the Evangelist presents a buoyant church that is
ready and poised for the demanding narrative of the book of Acts to follow.

FIRST LESSON: ACTS 1:1-11

The first paragraph of the book of Acts picks up the story of Luke 24
and reiterates the same themes (vv. 1-5). The first paragraph summarizes
the "first book," the Gospel (cf. v. 1). That first book concerns all that

Jesus "began to do and teach," until he was "taken up," that is, his whole
life story. Reference is made to the postresurrection experiences and the
"proofs" given of Jesus' resurrection (v. 3). The church, as we have seen
it in Luke 24, waits in Jerusalem for the promise of power to be fulfilled
(vv. 4-5).

The narrative quickly provides us with the matrix for the stunning narrative to follow. Now the narrative account advances (vv. 6-11). This unit
consists in three speeches, by the apostles, by Jesus, and by "two men,"
and a brief narrative statement which corresponds to the narrative closure
of Luke 24:50-53. It would be possible to preach a sermon on this series
of three speeches.

1. The *speech of the apostles* is a quest for certitude (v. 6). The question
they ask Jesus echoes the dispute of Luke 22:24-27 (cf. Mark 10:35-45).
The disciples-become-apostles still do not understand what Jesus is about.
They have misconstrued the intention of Jesus; moreover, they want a
timetable and concrete certitude. They want a piece of Jesus' future given
into their control.

2. *The answer of Jesus* is no response to their question of certitude;
instead of certitude, Jesus promises them power (vv. 7-8). First, Jesus
makes a negative response (v. 7). God keeps for God's own self the times
and seasons, and will not yield. Second, Jesus makes a positive response
(v. 8). The church wants certitude; it is offered power. The power promised
is of the Spirit. That power will authorize and compel testimony about the
gospel. Luke lays out the design of the book of Acts and his theory of the
missionary activity of the church (v. 8). He shows how the church grew
into all the known world. The power promised by Jesus and given by the
Spirit is so elusive that it does not yield the certitude sought in v. 6. Rather,
this power sets the church on a course of risk, danger, and venture, enacting
in the world Jesus' new life, a new life that destabilizes all present forms
of life.

Verse 9 provides a narrative interruption to the sequence of three speeches, to report the departure of Jesus from the church. We have encountered
the understated language of "parted" (Luke 24:51), "taken up" (Acts 1:2),
and now "lifted up" (v. 9). In v. 11, Jesus is "taken up into heaven." For
us the problem may be the disposal of the body of Jesus. For the early
church, the claim (not problem) of the narrative is the exaltation of Jesus
into the regime of God. Jesus now enters the cosmic government of God
as the central authority. Ascent is elevation, that is, exaltation, coronation,
and enthronement. That is the reason the disciples' reaction at the end of

the Gospel of Luke is one of great joy. The ascension is not a physiological embarrassment, but a political enactment of Jesus' sovereignty.

3. *The third speech* is made by "two men" in white robes (vv. 10-11). These are the same two who announced the resurrection (Luke 24:4). Their appearance and speech in both cases indicates we are witnesses to an awesome theophanic event that is not to be explicated in any mundane categories. There is something transcendent, inscrutable, and holy about what happened to Jesus. As the two men had announced the new life of Jesus (Luke 24:4), so now they assert that Jesus reigns in heaven and will return again in power. As Jesus has gone to heaven to rule, so he will return to earth to rule.

This awesome narrative account may seduce us into two modes of interpretation. On the one hand, we can take it as a flat description and force upon the text an excessive literalness, as though this event belonged to a literary genre of "men ascending into the clouds." Or if that is too embarrassing, we may seek to explain. Either to reduce to a class of narratives, or to dismiss by explanation is a misrepresentation of the text. The mode of the text wants us to take the text on its own terms, to explain it by reference to nothing else, to discern here that holiness causes the trembling and transformation of the world. The early church bears witness to the reality that the very man Jesus now occupies a decisive place and role in the governance of God's world (see the assertion of Acts 17:31).

The text stops in the lectionary at just the right place. We are thus far only at Ascension in the church year, and there is a waiting. In the church's reckoning of time, the church waits ten days for Pentecost. It waits those ten days without power. In the text of Acts, the church waits all of chapter one. What matters is that the church waits under promise for the gift of power that it can receive from no other source.

The text staggers to find language adequate for what is promised to the church but not yet given. It dares to speak of power, but this odd power does not conform to any of our social scientific analyses of power. This is power from heaven, inscrutable, irresistible, power like the wind, power that gives energy, freedom, courage, authority, and healing, power to transform the world. There is an odd, dramatic slippage between the departure of Jesus and the invasion of God's Spirit. This is the moment between Luke and Acts, the moment between Ascension and Pentecost. It may also be the in-between moment in the contemporary church. The church has only the promise. That, however, is enough!

EPISTLE: EPHESIANS 1:15-23

The epistle reading is a grand, sweeping, elegant commentary on the ascension. Its rhetoric overflows in lyrical eloquence and abundance. This is a difficult statement to understand, because of its grammatical complexity, expressed in one long sentence. Because the statement is daringly doxological, this text likely should not be scrutinized in too much detail, but heard in its large, bold affirmation.

The paragraph is cast as a part of the genre of epistle and is the standard greeting of thanksgiving (vv. 15-16). The prayer, however, is not primarily thanksgiving. It is petition. The speaker petitions that the saints addressed will receive gifts from God, gifts of wisdom, revelation, knowledge, and enlightenment (vv. 17-18a). Then follow three statements making the knowledge anticipated more specific:

"that you may know,

what is the hope . . .

what are the riches . . .

what is the greatness of God's power in us" (vv. 18b-19).

These majestic words invite the church to be more aware of, more receptive to, more confident in the great gifts of faith. God grants to the church the gospel that makes a life of faith and love more complete. All of these gifts are given in God's great might (v. 19).

Now the hymn moves decisively to an eloquent christological affirmation (vv. 20-23). The place where God's might has done its work is in Christ. God has raised Christ. God has raised Christ from the dead. God has raised Christ to the governance of heaven (v. 20). The phrasing suggests that what Luke separates as Easter and Ascension is in this Pauline tradition treated as a single act of glorification.

The text ends with a lyrical celebration of the sovereign power of Jesus (vv. 21-23). It is Jesus who is

far above all rule, authority, power, dominion . . .

above every name in this age and the age to come . . .

all things are under his feet . . .

he is head over all things.

The language of "far above, above, under, over" is the language of sovereignty, exaltation, and glorification. Christ rules over "all, every, all things, all things." The language is extravagant, because the theological claim is extravagant. The language is sweeping in its claim because the new sovereignty of Jesus is sweeping in its scope.

At the end, the writer adds a wondrous note (vv. 22-23). This new governance is "for the church," which is Christ's body. The new governance is not turned over to the church, but the governance is for the sake of the church where Christ can be fully Christ.

This text in its wondrous daring invites a faith that is lyrical, that shows how the claims of the gospel completely displace our ways of ordering the world. At the center of the world is a new reality wrought through Jesus.

In this text there is no explicit reference to the "event" of ascension as in Luke 24 and in Acts 1. This epistle reading, however, is fully congruent with those texts. It voices the same themes of authority for Christ in heaven and power for the church on earth. Thus the ascension is not a "mythological" statement about what happened to the body of Jesus. It is rather a doxological affirmation that the world has been reorganized, and the church is offered (promised) God's irresistible power of newness. On Ascension Day, the church is invited away from its routines and conventions to face the gift of new life that invites the church to a new way in the world, to a new, glad loyalty toward Jesus who governs in power. The stretch of the Easter season is from the surprise of Easter to the awe of Ascension. The entire sequence concerns Jesus' new governance which is known, trusted, and served in the church.

The Seventh Sunday of Easter

Lutheran	Roman Catholic	Episcopal	Common Lectionary
Acts 1:8–14	Acts 1:12–14	Acts 1:8–14	Acts 1:6–14
1 Pet. 4:12–17; 5:6–11	1 Pet. 4:13–16	1 Pet. 4:12–19	1 Pet. 4:12–14; 5:6–11
John 17:1–11	John 17:1–11a	John 17:1–11	John 17:1–11

GOSPEL: JOHN 17:1-11

These words of Jesus are part of the "Farewell Discourse." They are Jesus' words to and for the church as he leaves the church to claim his larger rule and glory. The words appropriately speak to us in the season between Ascension (Jesus' departure) and Pentecost (the coming of the Spirit). This "time between" may be ten days in the church year, but it may be experienced as much longer, as the church lives in a situation of seeming abandonment, uncertainty, and powerlessness. The text is addressed to the church in its dangerous, freighted moment of need.

The news to be preached in this "in-between" moment, is that the church is *prayed for*. This prayer has been prayed and continues to be prayed; for that reason the situation of the church is not as uncertain and powerless as it appears. The reality of this prayer changes the situation of the church on three grounds: *(a)* The prayer is uttered by the utterly faithful Jesus who loves the church as much as he commands the church; *(b)* the prayer is addressed to the utterly faithful God who hears and cares; *(c)* the substance of the prayer is that the church should be made whole, safe, and faithful. Because of *(a)* such a faithful speaker, *(b)* such a faithful listener, and *(c)* such a powerful petition, the situation of the church is completely different than we expected, even in its situation "in-between."

The prayer is dominated by the word "give." It is God who gives:

- God has given the Son power (v. 2).
- God has given the Son people (v. 2).
- God has given Jesus work to do (v. 4).
- God has given Jesus people (v. 6).
- God has given Jesus "everything" (v. 7).
- God has given Jesus words (v. 8).
- God has given Jesus people (v. 9).
- God has given Jesus a name (v. 11).

God powerfully, intentionally, and generously gives to Jesus. This relentless list of "give" establishes on the one hand *Jesus' sovereignty* (power, work, "everything," words, name). On the other hand, Jesus has entrusted to him by God this *special community*, which Jesus takes as his special charge to care for and protect (vv. 6, 9).

As God gives, so Jesus is the receiver of God's gifts and purposes. Jesus has had entrusted to him all the gifts that God chooses to give. This action of God and Jesus respectively, giving and receiving, evidences the communion, trust, and closeness between them. All that is in God's power is entrusted to Jesus' charge.

Jesus, however, not only receives. He also gives. What Jesus gives, he has received from God. Jesus gives to the church "words" (v. 8). These words, which may be variously commandments or promises, let the church know the truth. The truth given to the church is that Jesus is indeed the "one from God," who can be trusted as the one who gives life. In the gift of words, Jesus gives his own self to the church, even as God has given God's own self to Jesus.

In the midst of such giving and receiving, which reflects confidence, trust, and communion, we are given a new, good word about the church. This beloved community of Jesus is characterized in three ways:

1. The church is "in the world" (v. 11). The church must live in the midst of structures, power relations, and assumptions now operative in creation. The church is exposed and vulnerable, because "the world" is in principle hostile to the community that trusts and serves Jesus. The situation of the church is more exposed and vulnerable because Jesus is with God and is no more "in the world." The church is "in the world" without the company of Jesus. This prayer is uttered over a church Jesus loves, but a church that is profoundly at risk. It belongs to the character of the church in the world to be profoundly at risk.

2. The church, so vulnerable and exposed, is prayed for: "Keep them" (v. 11). God is asked by Jesus to be the God who guards, protects, and cherishes the church, even as God keeps Israel (cf. Ps. 121:7-8). Because God is this God, the protection of God overrides the threat of the world.

3. The petition is that the church "may be one" as God and the Son are one (v. 11). The oneness of God and Son is not a mechanical connection, but is a communion of full trust embodied in giving and receiving. The petition is that the church become a communion of full trust, embodied in giving and receiving.

FIRST LESSON: ACTS 1:6-14

On vv. 6-11 see "The Ascension of our Lord." The church has now witnessed the departure and enthronement of Jesus (v. 9). The believers have been summoned as witnesses (v. 8). They have been promised power (v. 8). They have been instructed to wait (cf. Luke 24:49). They have been assured of God's rule (Acts 1:11).

The new portion of the reading, not commented upon under the rubric of "The Ascension of our Lord," is in vv. 12-14. The church waits. They wait in Jerusalem where the newness will come. They wait in an upper room. They are all there, the disciples, and the women, and the family of Jesus. They are all there and they all wait. And they all pray. That is all we are told.

We are given a picture of a community now without its leader, but under the mandate of great promise. The church of Luke-Acts is not dismayed by Jesus' departure, but is filled with joy. The prayer of the church in this in-between season is joyous, buoyant, and expectant. The church is poised for new action in the world, ready for the power of God's sovereignty among them. The waiting of the church is focused, disciplined, and intentional.

The juxtaposition of this reading and the Gospel reading in John 17:1-11 is suggestive. In the Gospel reading, *Jesus prays* for the church. In this reading, *the church prays*. We are told of the prayer of Jesus but we are not told specifically of the church's prayer. The prayer prayed *for* the church by Jesus concerns protection and communion, and well-being in the midst of a hostile world. The prayer *by* the church might echo the prayer *for* the church. The church in-between might pray not to be hurt or seduced or domesticated by a hostile world. The church might pray for its oneness, and for power for the mission.

EPISTLE: 1 PETER 4:12-17; 5:6-11

The church in this season between Ascension and Pentecost is in jeopardy. It is without power and leaderless. It can only wait. It is set in the midst of an alien, hostile environment, protected only by God's watchful care. The "fiery ordeal" may take many forms, either by coercion and persecution, or by seduction (v. 12). The ordeal concerns pressure that talks the church out of its faith, its passion, its mission.

The "fiery ordeal," in its testing and its threat, may indeed cause suffering for the church. The notion of suffering for faith seems remote from our own social experience; the reality of such suffering, however, is not far removed in our contemporary world. In this text, the church under threat from the world is called to rejoice in suffering (v. 13). The church may rejoice in the midst of its suffering, because the church already is assured that Christ will triumph. The church does not believe that the present hostile power arrangements in the world will prevail or endure, because God's intent is of another kind. The joy to which the church is summoned is rooted in a deep and abiding certitude about Christ's rule that the world does not acknowledge but cannot nullify. The church knows something the world does not suspect. It knows of Christ's coming rule.

The sufferings proper to the church, however, are of a very specific kind (vv. 15-16). There are sufferings to be avoided and sufferings to be embraced. This summons to Christian suffering is no warrant for unworthy behavior which rightly brings the judgment of society (v. 15). Such suffering is to be avoided, for the church is to live above reproach. Thus, when the church is reproached, it must be for the right reasons, for reasons of faith and obedience, for reasons of embrace of the rule of Christ in a world where other powers imagine they rule. There will be a "revealing" in time to come (v. 13). There will be a breakthrough *(kairos)* for the claim and reality of the gospel. The rule of Christ will be a decision against every form of alienation, against every alternative way in the world. The church's proper suffering is for its embrace of that coming rule.

The argument of this text is thoroughly evangelical; it is rooted in the good news of Jesus' story of death and resurrection. There is a time of suffering for the church as for Jesus; there is a time of glory for the church as for Jesus (4:13). There is a time for humbling and for being exalted for the church as for Jesus (5:6). The people in this text, it is asserted, live at the "full time" when humbleness turns to exaltation, when suffering is overridden by joy.

The specific time of Christ's coming rule does not matter (cf. Acts 1:7). What counts is that the church keep faith in its hope. What matters is that the church understand its true situation, not only "in the world," but beset by "your adversary" who wants to make the church prey for devouring (5:8). This imagery may offend us. We are accustomed to imagine that the church is set among various choices and options, and we need only choose among them. Such a perception suggests that we have within our power to choose whatever we decide to do. Such a view of our situation, however, is an illusion; there are powerful forces that work against the church's embrace of the freedom of the gospel.

The church has freedom for its faith, not by easily choosing, but by struggling with the dangers and demands of the gospel. The writer of this epistle entertains no illusions and wants the church to face reality. There are indeed "powers and principalities" which work against our embrace of the gospel. The image of "your adversary" asserts the powerful, crucial recognition that the community of the gospel has deadly opposition which may have worldly manifestations, but is deeply rooted in a more cosmic, alien power. The church, even in middle North America, is beset by forces that do not want the life-giving power of the gospel set loose in society.

The church is called to resist the power of such pressure (5:9). The assault of evil is multifaceted—it may be coercion, persecution, or seduction. Conversely, the resistance may take many forms. We can imagine that in the Acts narrative, the primary weapon of resistance in the church is prayer. Here, in this text, it is an act of resistance not to be talked out of suffering, not to imagine that suffering is exceptional and to be avoided, but comes with the territory of faith. It is an act of intentional resistance to recognize that the claims of the gospel set us at odds with the world around us. We may be prepared for the hostility that serious faith evokes.

This text is utterly convinced that suffering for faithfulness will be followed by glorification, that humbleness will be succeeded by exaltation. It will all happen in "due time" (5:6). It will happen in "a little while" (5:10). In that breakthrough of God's power and God's sovereignty, God will restore, establish, and strengthen. "In a little while," the fullness of God's power and life-giving way will be granted. The church lives in an ominous hour, but it is the hour just before God's inbreaking.

Admittedly the framing of the argument in these texts strikes us as strange and perhaps old-fashioned. The church prays expectantly in Acts (Acts 1:14), Jesus acknowledges "the hour" in the Gospel reading (John 17:1). The epistle speaks of "a little while" (1 Peter 5:10). All these texts speak of the church at risk, being kept by the power of God who is about to do a new thing. The texts are all invitations to hope and expectation, living in the present, on the bet of what God will soon enact.

All such language of what is "at hand" (cf. Mark 1:15) seems remote from a church as settled as is the U. S. church. The church is experienced among us as a given social institution in a guaranteed social setting. Moreover, our theological reflection for the last decades has reduced eschatological hope in the church to a fantasy embraced only by religious freaks. It is for these reasons difficult to preach such texts where the church senses no jeopardy, waits with very little passion, embraces little moral urgency, and does not notice any in-breaking moment of God's *kairos*.

The sermon, I submit, could articulate the situation of the church in categories of risk. The community of faith then as now, is indeed in jeopardy. We are slow to imagine "your adversary," reluctant to notice that the adversary would like to talk us out of the suffering that belongs to faithful life in the world.

In the face of such a social circumstance, the texts make powerful affirmations. When the faithful church is put at risk and faces suffering, the breakpoint of exaltation is near. The texts may cause the church to notice its own moment of "in-between." In light of the power of the adversary (1 Peter 5:8), we see why the church prays (Acts 1:14), and why the church is prayed for (John 17:9).

The danger in which the church stands is matched and overmatched by the promise of the texts. It is remarkable that the text can look so squarely at the threat, and while looking, the epistle can assert: "Cast all your anxieties on God, for God cares for you (1 Peter 5:7). The God to whom Jesus prays in John 17 does indeed care. God cares for the church; that assurance gives the church courage to face the risks of the gospel.

The Day of Pentecost

Lutheran	Roman Catholic	Episcopal	Common Lectionary
Joel 2:28–29	Acts 2:1–11	Acts 2:1–11	Acts 2:1–21 *or* Isa. 44:1–8
Acts 2:1–21	1 Cor. 12:3b–7, 12–13	1 Cor. 12:4–13	1 Cor. 12:3b–13 *or* Acts 2:1–21
John 20:19–23	John 20:19–23	John 20:19–23	John 20:19–23 *or* John 7:37–39

FIRST LESSON: ACTS 2:1-21

The church had been promised power (1:8), but had been given no timetable (1:7). The church waited, in the meantime praying (1:14). Then suddenly, inexplicably, what was promised happened!

The event of Pentecost in Acts 2, like the resurrection occurrence in the Gospel narrative, can only be taken on its own terms. It cannot be explained in terms of anything else. It is not a happening that can be subsumed under a larger genre. Pentecost is an "originary event," originating the church. The narrative report of this chapter is cast as a "theophany," a narrative which bears witness to the shattering invasion of God's sovereignty, power, and purpose. The history of the church begins in an irruption of God's awesome holiness. The rest of the story of the church is a response to that unutterable event, wrought in God's massive, majestic freedom.

The happening is described in awed and awesome language (vv. 1-4). This language does not invite us to explanation, but to wonder. What happened was an invasion of power "from heaven," as forceful and as inscrutable as the wind (v. 2). Like the wind, one can only see the outcome of the irruption. The descriptive account here is not precise and technical. What happened is "like" wind, "like" fire. The narrative does not report on wind and fire, but something like that which defies characterization. Such a religious moment is not available for exact reportage. The experience outruns our ability to describe. What is required for such a retelling is the language of vision, allusion, and imagination.

The allusive character of the narrative of Pentecost is evident in the double use of the word "tongue." There were "tongues as of fire" (v. 3), which would seem to describe daring flames. These "tongues as of fire" came to rest on each member of the community in waiting. The shift from v. 3 to v. 4 is drastic. The word "tongue" is used a second time, but now the use is not allusive, but concrete. Now the word refers to speech. It is the "tongue of fire" which results in the "tongue of speech." Both tongues, of fire and of speech, are gifts of the invading, inscrutable wind of God.

The promise of the departing Jesus has been kept. Power has been given. It is such power that every normal category has been shattered. We are at a staggering point of new beginning. We are invited to awe, for who would have thought the power of God would create a new "speech situation"! Both speaking and hearing now occur in ways that the world had not experienced! This is indeed a new thing.

The response to the intrusion of God's wind is a response of wonder and cynicism (vv. 5-13). *The response of wonder* is framed by a literary inclusio of bewilderment, amazement, and wonder (vv. 6-7) as well as amazement and perplexity (v. 12). The ones to whom the invasion happened did not understand what had happened to them. The events are real; no one, however, knows what the events mean or what they require. The interpreter must take care not to know more than the text, but to let the dismay and astonishment of the text prevail in interpretation.

The wonder is that the Galileans (those closest to Jesus) speak their own language and all the others, that is, the whole world gathered in Jerusalem, hear and discern (vv. 7-8). All the barriers are broken. This is real, live speech, genuine communication. The speech in tongues does not obfuscate, but it communicates. It does not set up barriers but it breaks them down. The subject of the speech is "the mighty works of God" (v. 11). On the one hand, the phrase "mighty works of God" suggests the whole memory of Israel's faith as it is reflected in Stephen's subsequent sermon (7:2-53). The book of Acts keeps in purview this entire canonical recital of Israel. On the other hand, the phrase may suggest a recital of the events around

Jesus concerning his death and resurrection (cf. Luke 24:18-21). These events are now preeminently "God's mighty deeds."

Either way, the subject of the new speech of the church is a testimony to God's intrusive, transformative acts that have indeed turned the world upside down (Acts 17:6). The speech of the empowered church bears witness to the mighty acts. The wonder of God's life in Israel and among the nations begins in new speech. Such speech is followed by a series of actions which make new life possible.

The nations are enabled, by the power of God's Spirit, to hear, understand, embrace, and participate in the normative account of God's miracles wrought in these recited events (vv. 8-11). The communication that happened on that day in Jerusalem defies explanation. The text offers none nor should the preacher. What we would judge impossible is made possible by the power of God.

Most people, according to the narrator, accepted the events with wonder and amazement. They did not understand, but they accepted (v. 12). Others, however, *responded in cynicism* (v. 13). They refused to see in the speech event a mighty deed of God. The event was too outrageous. They explained away the powerful coming of the Spirit of God. By categorizing the new speech event as a scandal of drunkenness, they eliminated the authority of the Spirit and were able to contain the new power in old discernments. They received the "originary event" of God's coming according to more manageable categories. The wind of God is thereby domesticated. It then holds neither promise nor threat.

That response of cynicism, however, evokes from Peter a *bold theological interpretation* of the events just characterized (vv. 14-36). Peter rejects the explanation of drunkenness (v. 15). His alternative explanation begins not with words of his own, but only by quoting Scripture. The new speech event of Pentecost is an actualization of the "last day" anticipated by the prophet Joel (Joel 2:28-32). The poem from Joel explicates the odd communication made possible by the Spirit. The poem of Joel (as Peter's explication of the event) is in three parts:

1. The last days, the end of present realities, are marked by the invasion of God's Spirit (vv. 17-18). That powerful, transformative, sovereign, destabilizing presence of God will liberate all members of the community from a closed, fated practice of reality. Not only will language be loosened, but there will also be a liberation of discernment, perception, and epistemology. The Spirit of God permits all members of the community to see, know, and speak differently. There will be prophecies, visions, dreams.

These terms are all parallel, referring to *alternative* speech and discernment, outside all controlling conventions. All parts of the community, old and young, female and male, sons and daughters, manservants and maidservants, are invaded by the new possibility of fresh discernment and articulation. Nothing in the community is left unvisited, settled, unempowered, unauthorized, unliberated. All are changed for the newness God gives.

2. The spirit brings wonders and signs filled with threat and danger (vv. 19-20). The ominous catalog of blood, fire, smoke, and darkness suggests that the old world is under heavy assault. This assaultive rhetoric asserts that the wind of God (as it created the world in Gen. 1:2) will now *un*-create the world (cf. Jer. 4:23-26). An end to the known world is matched by a new speech situation, in which a new world comes unfettered and unqualified by what has been. New speech permits a new world, underived from what has been. Neither old speech nor the old world will now have any power. All that is old is placed in profound danger. The ones who dream, prophesy, and envision are the ones who have been torn loose from what is old for the sake of the newness that God now gives.

3. The final days will be days of severe judgment. The name of Jesus, however, can save (v. 21). Indeed, his is the only name, the only power, the only person that can save.

The wonder of new speech (vv. 6-11) and the interpretive poem from Joel (vv. 17-21) do not easily cohere. There is nothing in the speech event itself that bespeaks world-ending. The new speech threatens, but the "mighty deed of God" characteristically saves. Peter's exposition of the event through the Joel passage asserts the two-sidedness of Pentecost. The Spirit makes newness possible! The Spirit jeopardizes all that is old.

EPISTLE: 1 CORINTHIANS 12:3b-13

The gift of the Spirit of the church is not a passing event. Pentecost persists. The gift of the Spirit transforms the life of the church in decisive and enduring ways. It is the gift of the Spirit that lets the church make its primal confession. It is by the Spirit that the church is able to confess, "Jesus is Lord" (v. 3). It is the Spirit that gives the church faith to believe and courage to confess. Indeed, the church is a creature and creation of the Spirit. Pentecost thus is not a day simply to remember an odd, inexplicable event. It is also an occasion to acknowledge that God's Spirit generates life and enables ministry in the church in the present.

In his epistle, Paul addresses a church that is in deep tension (cf. 1:10-17). The church is beset both by party spirit and by competition among forms of ministry. These tensions endanger the unity and faithfulness of the church.

Paul speaks as a witness against those dangers. He attests that the capacities necessary to the church and evident in the church are not autonomous, not self-devised or self-possessed; they are gifts, all given from the same source, all given for the same purpose (v. 4). The single source of all the gifts is the Spirit. The single purpose of all the gifts is to enhance the rule of Jesus. The Spirit enables the confession that Jesus is Lord (v. 3). In no element of its life is the church a self-starter. All comes from the generous giving of the Spirit who is God.

Verses 4-11 are an expository comment on vv. 1-3. We may observe three items in the commentary that inform the church. First, the formula of vv. 4-6 is cast in inchoate trinitarian language: "same Spirit, same Lord, same God." The Spirit is related to gifts; the Lord is the one to be served; God is the one who inspires gifts. Thus the gifts are fully connected to the reality of God. The gifts come out of God's generosity; the gifts are intended for glad service to God. They are from God and for God.

Second, after the trinitarian allusion, the passage is dominated by the relentless reiteration of "same Spirit" (vv. 4, 8, 9, 11), and the parallel phrase, "one Spirit" (v. 9). All gifts come from a single, holy, life-giving source. Obviously, such gifts cannot be intended for competing, private, autonomous purposes, nor set over against each other.

Third, the inventory of gifts includes the large range of dimensions of the community (vv. 8-10). These several functions include utterance, faith, healing, miracles, prophecy, ability to distinguish spirits, and speaking in tongues.

The problem which concerns Paul is an old, yet contemporary issue in the church. The problem is the connection between *one Spirit* who gives gifts and *many gifts* that may even seem not related to each other. The problem has two dimensions. On the one hand, there may be autonomous thinking about the gifts; they are regarded as property and possession of one's self, underived, and therefore not accountable. On the other hand, the gifts may be perceived as though derived from different sources and therefore the gifts may be used for different purposes, even cross-purposes.

Skills and gifts in the church are in fact gifts given for the service of God. For that reason, the church community has priority over the individual person in the utilization of gifts. Thus, initiative for the use of gifts belongs not to the individual, but to the community to which the individual owes allegiance and is bound to make response.

It is odd that the notion of Spirit often becomes a divisive factor in the life of the church. The witness of the Acts narrative is exactly the opposite. The Spirit gathers the church to be one community, engaged in mutual sharing of gifts. Paul's practical affirmation readily derives from the theological claims of the Acts narrative.

GOSPEL: JOHN 20:19-23

See "The Second Sunday of Easter" on these verses. The risen Jesus comes among his disciples. Jesus came among them through closed doors (v. 19). When the disciples see his wounded hands and side, they know it is he, and they rejoice (v. 20). In vv. 19-20, the narrative establishes both that this is the same Jesus who was crucified, and that he now moves among his followers in inscrutable and powerful ways.

Jesus' greeting to the church, twice repeated, is "Peace be with you" (vv. 19, 21). This is Jesus' characteristic and magisterial greeting. It is speech that changes the circumstance of the church. "Peace" is what Jesus embodies and what he brings. He comes to a church beset by turmoil, fear, and confusion. Jesus' presence, his speech, and his assurance transform the church. The peace of Jesus leads to his sending of the disciples (v. 22). His assurance of peace is not an end in itself, but a step toward command (v. 22). The church is not sent out powerless or resourceless. It is not sent under its own stem. It is sent with the wind of God to embody the peace Jesus gives (v. 22).

The power of the church is enormous. The church's business is the administration of human sin, either to forgive or to retain (v. 23). This sentence reflects the sacramental awareness of the church and its handling of the sacramental power entrusted to it. The focus of the church's trust is direct and concise. Its agenda is the administration and processing of sin which divides, alienates, and destroys. The text might lead to reflection upon the church's engagement with the reality of sin, its power to forgive, and its grounds for refusal to forgive.

In these brief verses, we are provided an epitome of ecclesiology: The church is greeted in peace, set in mission, empowered by the Spirit, and authorized against the reality of sin. The church is given an awesome responsibility, matched by awesome power. The *new life of Jesus* in Easter leads to a *new power for the church* in Pentecost. The risen Christ authorizes transformative faith and ministry.